Baghdad, Iraq

Kuwait City, Kuwait

Indian
Ocean

Mama & Boris's Journey Home

Mama & Boris

★★WELCOME HOME★★

Mama & Boris

How a Sister's Love Saved a Fallen Soldier's Beloved Dogs

Carey Neesley *with* Michael Levin

Reader's Digest

The Reader's Digest Association, Inc.
New York, NY

A READER'S DIGEST BOOK

Copyright © 2013 The Reader's Digest Association, Inc.

Front cover, title page, and dog tags photos: © Amanda Friedman. Bottom back case photo: © Molly Wald. Interior photos as copyrighted. All other photos courtesy of the author.

Library of Congress Cataloging-in-Publication Data
Neesley, Carey.
  Welcome home, Mama and Boris : how a sister's love saved a fallen soldier's dogs / by Carey Neesley ; with Michael Levin
      pages cm
  ISBN 978-1-62145-115-0 (alkaline paper) -- ISBN 978-1-62145-116-7 (epub)
  1. Neesley, Carey. 2. Neesley, Peter, -2007. 3. Brothers and sisters--Michigan--Biography. 4. Dog rescue--Iraq. I. Title.
  CT275.N4234 2013
  920.0774--dc23

                                            2013014572

We are committed to both the quality of our products and the service we provide to our customers. We value your comments, so please feel free to contact us.

      The Reader's Digest Association, Inc.
      Adult Trade Publishing
      44 South Broadway
      White Plains, NY 10601

For more Reader's Digest products and information, visit our website:
      www.rd.com (in the United States)
      www.readersdigest.ca (in Canada)

Printed in the United States of America
1 3 5 7 9 10 8 6 4 2

★

This book is dedicated in loving memory of
Army Sgt. Peter C. Neesley
&
Every warrior who gave his or her life
in Operation Iraqi Freedom and Enduring Freedom
so all can stand free.

★

If I can stop one heart from breaking,
I shall not live in vain;
If I can ease one life the aching,
Or cool one pain,
Or help one fainting robin,
Unto his nest again,
I shall not live in vain.

—EMILY DICKINSON, "NOT IN VAIN"

Contents

"If ever there is tomorrow when we're not together, there is something you must always remember. You are braver than you believe, and stronger than you seem, and smarter than you think. But the most important thing is, even if we're apart, I'll always be with you."

—Christopher Robin to Pooh, A. A. Milne

Carefree

We are together.

In Southfield, Michigan, outside our family's ranch house, we are enjoying the sun streaming through the trees on a fine afternoon. We are playing in the garden, running past the flowerbeds and into the meadow. We roll down the hill, newly fallen leaves crunching underneath us, as we go past the trunks of apple and cherry trees. We are laughing, breathless, and happy, left to our own devices with no one but our dogs to watch us romp. We make up games and keep each other company. I am four, and Peter is two, and we are together.

This is many years before I would bury him, my baby brother. Years before we would grow up, before he would never get old. We didn't know that day what the future would hold for us; that he would come to be caring and kind, wise beyond his years. That I would watch him learn and struggle, fail and fall, rise

and rest, forever at peace. That he would be like a father to my child, a guiding light to us both. That long
after he left this world, he would still be with me, his
legacy alive and well.

We couldn't know about the attacks, about the
war. We couldn't know about the homecoming—
about the news vans that would circle my small house
one day, about the red, white, and blue balloons that
would float in front of a "Welcome Home" banner—a
different sort of celebration.

For now, we don't know any of this.

We just know we are together, and that today is a
good day.

ONE

Black Sheep

My life in Southfield starts out idyllic, carefree. Like most children, I'm happy and content. My family is everything to me. We're lucky enough to have a close connection with our extended family, too, and my brother Peter and I spend a lot of time with our grandparents, aunts, uncles, and cousins. In the summers, we go up north to spend quality time together, swimming in the lake. Holidays, we go up there, too, huddling close in a cozy cottage, warm against the winter nights. Birthday parties and family gatherings are big-to-do events, not to be missed. My memories are like photo albums, with no unhappy moments pressed between the pages.

Peter, born two years after me but only two days earlier in January, is my best friend from the beginning. We are like twins: We look the same, talk the same, act the same, are the same. I feel so grateful for him and all the time we spend together playing in the woods outside our house with our Irish setter and springer spaniel, Casey and Arrow, by our side.

Our family is growing. Our parents tell us that we will have a little brother soon, Theodore. He is named after our grandfather—my hero, and Peter's. Our grandfather is a judge on the circuit court and the beloved patriarch of our little clan. More than anything, he believes in family, and that comes through in the way that we all see each other all the time, the way that we are there for each other, the way that, if you miss a birthday party or a gathering, you are in big trouble.

I know a little bit about his past, and soon, it would all make sense to me—why our family is so close when I know that sometimes other families aren't. Before he grew up, before he was a judge, Grandpa Bohn was an orphan. He had no one. When he was about eight years old, he was adopted by a family, not for want of love or for want of another child—another voice in the house like our new baby brother would be—but to work on a farm. His hands grew rough from the hard labor, which he'd have to start before even the sun was awake. He came down with pleurisy, a lung disease, and would forever be behind in school. Things weren't easy for him like they were for Peter and me, and though I didn't understand much back then, I understood this.

Fortunately, my grandfather met my grandmother

in high school, and they married and moved to Detroit. He worked as a butler and she as a maid, for the big houses in Grosse Pointe, the upper-middle-class suburb where people had money and families were perfect. They scrimped and saved, and he went to law school at night after working all day. By the time he finally started work in a law firm, they had four daughters—my mom and her three sisters—and he could stand back and look at the dreams he'd built, brick by brick. My grandparents both fought for civil rights: he on the legal side, and she for the women's lib movement. One day, he bought one of the big houses in Grosse Pointe and raised his family there. We thought the world of him, so when our parents tell us that because our family is growing, it is time to move to Grosse Pointe, we are happy to go, even if it means leaving behind our magical meadow and forest, our very own woods. I'll find the best places on the playground, so that I can show him and Ted, too, when he's old enough.

When we get to Grosse Pointe, it is time for me to start kindergarten. I am sad to leave Peter behind, but I am excited to finally start school. I want to learn everything about our new school so that when Peter starts, we can pick up where we left off—spending our days together. I will learn the layout of the building, the names of the teachers, the route I'd take to school—just a one-block walk from our house.

But things are changing, and not just the size of our family, or where we live. Our parents are arguing a lot, and looking back later, I would realize that things had started to fall apart even as we were building our new home together. For six more years, life goes on like this, and Peter and I grow closer than ever as we try to protect each other from what is going on around us.

School is changing, too, and not in a good way. When I started out in kindergarten, the kids were nice; but over time, something shifts. I know that the neighborhood is full of so many big houses, fancy cars, and dads with important jobs. But our father is an insurance salesman, and even though he works just as hard as the other fathers, we don't have as much money as those families do. We don't know this, and we are happy just the same—we have each other, and we've always known that family is what matters most. But as Peter and I get older, the kids treat us differently, laugh at us, and pick on us. The teachers are no better; they must know we're different, too. I'm not sure how to fix it, and it's not getting better.

At home, things aren't getting better, either. We know that our parents are not happy, and when I am in sixth grade—twelve years old—they sit us down to tell us that my father has met someone else, someone he works with. It's not our fault. They will still love us the same. We will stay in our same house, go to our same school. Everything will stay the same, except everything will change.

★ ★ ★

Peter and I are growing older now, getting into more trouble. We were used to a tight-knit, picture-perfect life, but that was gone. We feel lost, even though we have each other. Our parents' divorce is bitter, and although they're doing the best they can, they can't help but try to turn the kids against the other parent.

Even though it should have been our own private trauma, news of the separation rattles around Grosse Pointe like a gunshot. In our small community, the divorce is tantamount to a scandal. Seemingly overnight, we become the black sheep of the neighborhood—my parents both lose their friends, who feel too awkward to stick around, and the children of those friends, who were our friends, are suddenly nowhere to be found. Peter and I feel like we're being punished for something that's completely out of our control and not our fault. Teachers start to write us off as being from a broken home, and we begin to act the part.

Our father continues to provide for us as best he can, but to keep two homes running, my mother has no choice but to return to school and then to work. She becomes a social worker, and I watch her with admiration: She's taking care of other people with problems all day and then comes home to us. I know she is devastated by the divorce, and so I understand when Peter and I are left on our own. With little Ted to take care of, I try to step into the role of the mother and Peter into the role of the father. We are playing house in our broken home, doing the best we can, just like our parents.

Since my mother is at school or work most of the time, we become latchkey kids. It becomes clear to all the other troublemakers in our school that our house is the place to hang out. We start to get drunk, to try drugs. At school, nobody wants to reach out to us and let us know that we're not alone in what we're going through, and the teachers continue to write us off. I'm doing okay, but Peter's grades are slipping. He's worried he isn't doing well enough to make much of his life, even though he has the brightest light burning inside him; everyone he meets loves him instantly. He is blossoming into a talented musician: He has taught himself the guitar, and started to write beautiful, sad songs down in our basement. Still, he feels like he doesn't deserve much, and I wonder if this is the toll the divorce has taken on him.

Our family is about to grow and change again several years later when I get in over my head with a boy who is not ready for the responsibilities that we unwittingly fall into. After a few months of feeling sick and sluggish, I go to see the doctor, who performs an ultrasound.

I am three months pregnant. I watch in awe of the undulating mass on the screen: a little blip of white sloshing around in the fluid in my abdomen. "Can you hear that?" the doctor asks.

At first, I can't hear anything but the pounding of my own heart. But as I stare at the screen and sit in the quiet dark of the exam room, it starts to get clearer: his heartbeat. That is my son. I know a couple of things right then: I know that I will keep this baby, will raise him and love him forever. And I know that I'm probably going to have to do it on my own.

I nod and tell the doctor that I can hear it. I am in love with my son, and I don't know if it's some strange, roundabout way of the world offering me redemption for my own broken home, but I know that I will make a wonderful mother for this baby. I am going to have a chance to build my own family.

I go home that day knowing that I will have to make some changes in my life. No more drinking and no more drugs, certainly, but I'm going to have to make a proper home for this baby, for this boy, my boy. I'm going to have to grow up and find my way back to the right path, starting with going to college. I know that my son's father, though around for now, probably won't be staying for long.

When I share the news with my parents, they are

incredulous. "You're not ready to be a mother," they say matter-of-factly, pressing me to consider adoption.

Peter sits quietly, but I know he's already made up his mind, too. "You can do this," he tells me, looking sure and strong, there to catch me if I fall. "I know you're going to be a great mother. I believe in you."

It is always like that with Peter—he is my rock.

I'm living in a small apartment on my own as I prepare to start my family. I half-heartedly look at places to live with my boyfriend and the baby, but nothing seems to come together. Peter quickly steps up to the plate—and then some—when my boyfriend takes off; he's there the night that my son is born. I notice that Peter has truly become a man, even though he's only six months out of high school.

I name the baby Patrick, and we move back into my mother's house. It's crowded with Ted and Peter at home, but I will need my mom's support as I start this new journey. I know that Peter feels the same way I do about Patrick; I know he sees it as our chance to have a perfect family. Not the picture-perfect Grosse Pointe family, but family members who love each other unconditionally and who stick together no matter what. Peter does everything he can to make this possible. He stays up in the middle of the night with Patrick, taking shifts feeding him so that I can get some sleep before class or work.

Even though I have the support of my mother,

who puts a roof over my head, I know that I need to contribute to the household finances and build up a nest egg. I start out by waitressing for a while, and then become a receptionist at a doctor's office. It's hard work, especially on top of all the time I have to spend at school, where I'm studying to be a social worker. I am inspired by my mother and my childhood hero—my grandfather. I want to work with the elderly.

There are many sleepless nights, but I have the most beautiful baby boy. Even though he's not quite a year old, I can see so much of Peter in Patrick—his personality, his smile, his sense of humor. The two are inseparable, just as Peter and I had been growing up. For what feels like the first time since those long-ago days in the yard in Southfield, I feel hopeful—even happy—about the future.

TWO

A New Family

I can't believe how fast this first year has gone. It is early in 2000, Patrick is now a year and a half old, and he continues to be the light of my life. I've saved up a little money and move us into a small apartment near my mother's home, and my parents are generous with their time, coming over to babysit Patrick while I'm at school or work. But most of all, Peter is there to help us, and apart from me, he is Patrick's whole world.

But Peter still struggles to figure out what he wants to do with his life, and I know that, no matter how much he loves us, he needs to move on, to have his own life. Though he tries a few courses at the community college and takes odd jobs here and there, nothing really seems to stick. I can tell he's dissatisfied and looking for something bigger. He continues to write and play music down in the basement with his friends, a place they've dubbed "The Weasel Den." It's one of the only places he seems happy, playing and singing and devoting hours to putting graffiti up on the walls after securing my mother's permission. But there's a darkness to his music, something that betrays the heartache, the longing, the emptiness brewing inside of him. I try to convince him that, despite what he might think, he's incredibly smart and talented, and would be a great fit for college. If he went to college, I argue, he'd be able to find a job he liked. He does me the favor of listening, but I can tell his mind is somewhere else.

Soon, Peter sits us down to share some news. He has decided to enlist in the Army. We are hesitant to feel good about the decision; Peter has always been accident prone—how could we let our son, our brother, our best friend go off to fight? We remind ourselves, though, that the country isn't at war with anyone, and concede that it's a good thing for Peter. It will give him some direction, and maybe he'll use it as a stepping stone to a career or better yet, to college. Reluctantly, we accept the decision, but then offer our support wholeheartedly. He has always been there for us, and we have no intention of being anything less than completely supportive of him.

Before he reports to boot camp at Fort Knox in Kentucky, I buy him a small gold charm: a four-leaf clover, for luck. I tell him that he needs to keep it with him at all times, as a reminder that I will always be with him. It gives me some comfort to know that, through this gift, I will be watching over my baby brother, just like when we were young—before he started to watch over me. I want him to think of me and to keep himself as safe as possible. He puts the charm on his chain with his dog tags.

I know it's hard for Peter to leave Patrick, in particular, and it's a blessing that Patrick is too young to understand what's going on. I tell him that his uncle will be back very soon, that he is off working. He misses Peter, but time passes differently for children. My days are spent worrying, although I ultimately find relief in the knowledge that Peter is not overseas; he is not at war; there are no trenches—not yet. He eventually is stationed at Fort Hood in Texas, where he trains as a paratrooper and a sniper. He writes to tell us of his adventures, like the time he gets bitten by a scorpion and the time he gets jet fuel dumped all over him. He sounds happy, though, and excited to be doing something with his life. I have to remind myself to be happy for him, too.

Time goes on, and Peter's letters, phone calls, and visits help us stay connected. Patrick is getting bigger by the day, it seems. On September 11, 2001, Patrick is nearly three, and I drop him off at his sitter's house. I enjoy the small amount of quiet time that I have before I have to rush off for class. The sky is blue, clear, calm.

I sit down in my classroom at Wayne State. Soon after class starts, people's phones start ringing, and news begins to trickle into the room. Something is not right, and there is tension and growing panic in the air. I'm not sure what's going on. Eventually, the professor rolls in a television and turns it on. My jaw drops and tears sting the back of my eyelids as I watch buildings on fire, planes crashing into the World Trade Center and the Pentagon. I'm not sure I truly understand what I'm seeing. I don't think any of us do.

"You all can leave," says the professor. "You don't have to stay here."

I walk into the bright morning not sure of what to do next. I remember that I need to return some textbooks, which cost a fortune, and I can't afford to not return the ones I don't need. I make my way to the campus bookstore, my feet on autopilot as my head buzzes with anxiety and fear. What does this mean? What will happen to Peter? Suddenly, the world seems more sinister, the future more bleak. I know that things will change for the brave men and women in the armed forces sooner than for the rest of us.

I pick up Patrick at the sitter's, and I'm still in shock. When we get home, I plop him in front of a kids' movie, and he sits, blissfully unaware of the world catching fire and tumbling down around us. In the next room, I turn on the news, and all I can think about is Peter. Why hasn't he called? Is he already somewhere and I don't know about it yet? Did something happen? Why isn't the phone ringing?

Suddenly, my prayers are answered, and the phone rings, its shrill cry piercing the air in the room. My mind tunes out the cartoons and the news and tunes in to Peter's voice. Is he scared? Is he safe?

"What happens now, Peter?" I ask.

"We go to war," he says.

I am quiet, the devastation choking me. "I'm scared. I don't want you to go."

"I love you, Care," is his only response.

★ ★ ★

For some reason, we are lucky, and Peter's unit never gets called up. President Bush declares war and rockets light up the sky over Baghdad, but Peter's unit stays stateside. Selfishly, I am happy; although other people's brothers and sisters start to die and return home in flag-draped caskets, my brother is safe in Texas. He works hard in the Army, preparing for the day that they will need him to join his new brothers and sisters. In his spare time, he works on his music, producing and recording two albums and playing in bars in neighboring Austin. His talent still amazes me, even from so far away.

In 2003, when his tour is up, he comes back home. I am ecstatic. I can finally see him, speak to him in person, hug him. I won't have to spend every minute in fear that he will be deployed overseas and put in imminent danger; he is right here. He tries to fit back into the civilian routine, taking classes at the college and playing with Patrick. But something is missing—something is not quite right. At night, he watches the news and quietly looks over letters from his friends in the Army. He keeps in touch with many of the men he met while in basic training and at Fort Hood and watches as they're deployed to Iraq. One night, he is visibly shaken and upset; when I ask him what's wrong, he tells me that one of his best friends has been killed in Iraq, leaving behind a wife and two kids.

I know better than to tell him I'm relieved it's not him. I stay quiet as he tries to find the words to voice his frustration. I know that Peter has a kind of survivor's guilt; he feels that if he had been there, he perhaps could have done something to prevent his friend's death. I suspect that we will lose him to the Army again soon, and it turns out to be only a matter of days. He ends up re-enlisting, keeping it a secret until the papers are already signed. He correctly guesses that we would have tried to talk him out of it.

A darkness falls over our family. We all have our own way with coping with Peter's decision: My father focuses on the well-deserved pride for his son, fighting for his country; my mother is stoic and strong, but I can tell she's worried underneath it all. We all try to keep a strong front, but after a lifetime of watching my family endure triumph and tragedy alike, I know how to read the signs—when they are having a bad day, when they are sad, when they are unsure. I am unabashedly a mess, wracked with grief in advance for all the uncertainty that is sure to follow. As the days pass, it seems undeniable: We worry that this time, we will not be as fortunate as we were the first time. I look outside at the world, and it's almost like I can't recognize it. We started our lives under blue skies—how did we end up here?

I feel it will take a lot more than a gold charm to keep my brother safe. I sit in the dark, in the quiet, and I pray.

THREE

It's Time

One day melts into the next. Weeks pass, then months, all marching lockstep toward the inevitable. Peter lets us know that he has been called up. I count my blessings that his first year will be spent at a base in Schweinfurt, Germany. We hear stories from him, mostly happy ones: He's so excited to explore Europe, traveling around the continent and making new friends, experiencing things that are so far away from our lives in Michigan. He drinks real German lager from steins shaped like boots and takes weekend trips to Paris. In one letter, he writes to tell us about participating in the running of the bulls in Spain, and while part of me cringes at the thought of Peter being chased by giant beasts driven by the instinct to gore him, the other part of me feels happy, alive, and free—like he has taken a piece of me with him on those adventures, like I am running the stony Spanish streets, too.

But there are things that Peter can't outrun—or

doesn't want to. After his tour in Germany, he returns to this side of the pond, to Fort Stewart in Georgia. Despite being offered a slot at Warrant Officer School at the base, which will keep him safe and stateside for the rest of his tour, Peter has an undeniable sense of duty and a saddened heart over the losses that he feels he could have prevented. So we are not surprised when word arrives—just a few months after he sets his boots back on American soil—that his night sky will soon be different, riddled not with starlight but gunfire; soon it will be his turn to defend our country, minute by minute, bullet by bullet. This time, we know that Peter will not be stationed nearby, or even in the relative safety of Europe. It feels real and unreal all at once; this can't possibly be happening to us, I think, while in the same breath lamenting the fact that it is. He is to report to Iraq, to Baghdad, to that dusty cradle of life that has for so many become an early grave.

I try my hardest to appreciate the positives in my life: that I still have time with Peter before he leaves, that I am raising a beautiful boy who is growing taller, stronger, and more like his uncle every day. I have been in a relationship for years with a friend of Peter's, a man I want to love and build a life with. I spend time looking at homes for us, hoping that one day we'll move out on our own and I'll get another chance to make a family for Patrick. This man and I get engaged, and soon I'm looking at wedding venues instead of houses. Peter is skeptical; he doesn't think this man is good enough for me, or that he will be the support that Patrick and I need. I wave him off, thinking I know better. He's leaving soon, and I don't want to be alone.

I focus on my studies, devoting as much time to my burgeoning career as I can. It's not easy being a single parent, but with Peter's help, I can see the light at the end of the tunnel. Soon, I will graduate with a master's degree in social work—the day before Peter is to be deployed, as it turns out. We argue about whether I will come down to Fort Stewart to see him off.

"Of course I'm coming," I tell him.

He is too proud of me to let me shake off this moment and spend it with him and miss getting my diploma in person up on that stage at Wayne State. "But you're graduating," he says.

Nothing could be further from my mind than all that pomp and circumstance. "Peter, don't be ridiculous. I'm coming to see you."

He cuts me off before I can argue further. I feel a deep-seated exhaustion start to creep into my spine, my limbs, my heart. He has made up his mind, and there's no turning back from that. "Fine," I relent, holding back tears. I don't want to fight with him, not when we have such few precious weeks left together. At this point, each minute seems to pass in triple time, in tune with the frantic beating of my heart.

Patrick is nine years old now, and he has gotten used to the idea that his Uncle Peter is a soldier in the Army, but I'm still not sure he knows exactly what that means. He doesn't know what goes on over there on the other side of the television screen after he goes to bed at night. I know he's heard little snippets about the towers, but nothing of the death toll—being in elementary school, he's been relatively shielded from the horrible truth of this war. I don't want him to know these things. I'm worried, and then angry, when I find him crying in his bedroom one night when I go to tuck him in.

"What's wrong?" I ask, expecting the usual boyhood answer—some slight that happened on the jungle gym during recess that day, some wound that needs a brightly colored Band-Aid and a kiss from mom.

"You know that Peter is going to war," he tells me, his blue eyes serious, sober, ringed with wet tears and dark circles.

My throat closes up. Who has he been talking to?

"Is he going to die?" he asks.

I take him in my arms and hold him tight, try to squeeze all the bad thoughts from his mind, thinking about the desert bogeymen he's imagining tearing his uncle limb from limb. For a long time, I don't say anything. I can't. Then I try to convince him that everything is going to be just fine, but I know I'm not just talking to him—I'm trying to convince myself, too.

Later, downstairs, I am shaking with rage as I pick up the phone to call Peter. In our years raising Patrick together, we've had a few dust-ups over parenting philosophy; it comes with the territory—I would feel I was right because I was Patrick's mother, and Peter would feel he was right because he was my big little brother. Peter is cooler, more laid back than I am—when Patrick wanted a Nerf gun, I tried to argue until I was blue in the face, but Peter just laughed it off. Boys will be boys, he told me, rolling his eyes. We always work it out because we both have Patrick's best interests at heart, but I am finding it hard to feel any equanimity about this situation. I am angry—not necessarily just at Peter, but also at the world, at the war, at the reality of what we will face when Peter steps onto that plane and out of our sight.

"What do you think you're doing?" I hiss into the phone through gritted teeth.

"Huh?" Peter is understandably taken aback.

"Patrick. What did you tell Patrick? Did you tell him you were going to die over there?"

Peter takes a moment to compose himself, the sigh from Fort Stewart trickling through the phone line and out the receiver in my kitchen in Michigan. "Carey, he needs to know," Peter says.

"He's a child," I insist. "Why would you tell a child such horrible things? There's no reason for him to be frightened."

Even as the words are spilling out of my mouth, I can hear how desperate I sound. Not for Peter to see my way of thinking, but for the words I'm saying to be true. "It's important for him to understand that I might not come back," Peter says.

"That's not going to happen."

"Carey—"

"No. You need to stop focusing on this idea that this is what is going to happen to you! It's going to be fine."

Peter gives up quickly when he sees how adamant I am. Maybe he even feels a little sad, a little sorry for me—his lost sister, so far away, with no idea what he's in for. No idea how to deal with what she knows, deep down, that he's in for. "Okay, Carey," he says, and lets it lie, this small comfort, the only kind he can give me now.

FOUR

Sundays

I'm trying to move on with my life, but it's hard. My relationship, which has always been somewhat tumultuous, hits a stumbling block. It's hard to focus on a wedding dress, catering decisions, and planning my future when my heart isn't in it. I'm too worried about Peter, and I'm less than enthralled with my fiancé these days—if it's support I need, I know I won't find it with him. Still, I am determined to make a safe, stable home for Patrick, especially after the turmoil of my own childhood. I start to insist that my fiancé come with me to look at houses in person, and for about six months, he goes along with it. But nothing is good enough, nothing welcomes us to start building our foundation, our life. I take him to house after house, and he hates each and every one, for reasons big and small. The kitchen counters, the cabinet hardware, the way the light falls on a certain swatch of carpet—anything is an excuse to keep us from beginning our lives together.

With Peter gone and getting settled in Iraq, I struggle to keep my feelings in perspective, my anxieties in check. I don't have the support of other military families to lean on—because Peter never let us come see him at any of his bases, opting instead to come home to Michigan, we didn't know anyone from that world and hadn't made any friends who could understand exactly what we were going through. Each member of our family tries to grasp on to their own normalcy, trying to move forward the best way they can. Every morning, although I wake up beside my fiancé and soon see my son's smiling face at the breakfast table, I can't shake the feeling that I am going through my days alone. Some days I am angry; some days I am worried; some days I cry constantly, inconsolable, for hours on end. I am at the same time a part of my own world and not—my mind floats elsewhere, far over the ocean, while my body sits at its desk, sees patients in hospice, makes dinner for my child.

I can see that my fiancé is losing his patience with my sorrow. The wedding planning brings added stress to our relationship, and he fights me on everything. Neither one of us has been married before. Even though I feel like, as a single parent, I've lived lifetimes and eons, I'm still young, only thirty. I still want a wedding with a pretty white dress, with my family by my side—nothing lavish, just something simple and all about love. I want to have that special day every girl dreams of, when all eyes are on her as she starts her future under the best of circumstances, the happiest hours. I'm aware it might be wishful thinking, especially since I am so torn up inside about Peter being at war.

Although he tries to shield me from what's going on, I do my best to keep up with the news, and spend time reading books on post-traumatic stress. I want to make sure that I can help him when he comes back, give him whatever he needs to re-adjust to our world. And even in the midst of my wedding angst, I have a glimmer of hope—Peter has promised that he has secured a leave for October so that he can attend the wedding. So even though it causes me pain to hear my fiancé insist that we should just go down to the courthouse and get it over with, rather than have a celebratory event, I can make it through the disappointment as long as I keep my eye on the silver lining: Peter will be home in October.

Back in Baghdad, Peter sets up a routine of calling us on Sunday mornings. Most of the time, especially in the beginning, we don't really know what to say to him—how can we possibly offer any comfort or have anything to talk about when we're living two very different lives, at opposite ends of the world? I think about the small talk that I have with my friends, the little gripes, the shared complaints, and how all of that seems almost laughably inconsequential in the face of what Peter is dealing with. Even though the idea of him being at war seems so unreal, in a way, it's more intense than anything that I would ever go through on a typical day at home in Michigan.

Still, despite any lingering strangeness, Sundays are always good days. We expect a call around the same time—ten or eleven o'clock for us, the middle of the night for Peter. Although he writes occasional letters and emails, these phone calls are our lifeline. We get a chance to talk to him and hear his voice, evidence that he's alive and doing well enough to speak. Sometimes he is too busy to talk long, or too exhausted. There are times when he is too sick to call, having contracted a horrible stomach virus from drinking bad water out in the desert. I try to understand the logistics that can easily prevent a soldier from calling home, but this does nothing to ease the lump in my throat every time we are left waiting for a call that never comes. Has something happened? Is he okay? Will the next knock at the door be accompanied by devastating news?

My fiancé starts to openly roll his eyes at my distress. "I bet Peter's not even in Iraq," he jokes, "he's probably just being dramatic."

I can't believe what I'm hearing, and a red rage mists over my eyes. I know he's just trying to assuage my fears, but I can't understand why anyone would even attempt to make light of a situation that has had all the light wrung from it. If I'm looking for support, this is the wrong man, I think, shutting myself down a little more, day by day. I'm building up walls so that I don't have to lean on him when I'm upset about Peter.

By the time summer comes around, it is hot in Michigan. These dog days seem to offer none of the cooling breezes that sometimes blow off the lakes and into our living room through the open windows. Patrick is out of school, trying to cool himself down with the neighborhood kids, running through lawn sprinklers and binging on sticky popsicles. But I know that this, like everything else, pales in comparison to the heat that chokes Peter's unit in Baghdad, which lingers there even long after the blistering sun has gone to bed. One day, a respite from the heat comes in the form of a quick afternoon rain shower, the water refreshing the scorched ground. I stand at my window and watch young children laughing, playing like Peter and I used to, carefree and soaking wet, jumping in puddles and drunk on summertime. The windows and walls between us aren't the only things that keep me from enjoying their moment; I am quietly crying, thinking of Peter stuck in a Humvee in the 130-degree heat. For Peter, there are no rain showers, no puddles.

My fiancé catches me crying and voices his displeasure before going about his business. Watching the kids playing in the rain, I slip my left hand into my pocket, where I use my fingers to swirl my engagement ring until it falls off my finger. I know that I am strong, that my life can hold more for me than a man who can't understand me, will never know me. Soon after, I call off the engagement, which comes as a surprise to no one, certainly least of all Peter.

My parents are so supportive of me, saying that they could tell that things weren't quite right and that if this isn't the right thing for me, I am doing the best possible thing by calling it off. They both remind me that I don't owe anyone any explanation, and that just because we announced the wedding didn't mean that I had to go through with it. Most of all, they say, Patrick and I will go on with our lives, and eventually I'll meet someone else.

Peter, for his part, is gracious on the phone, and holds back from telling me that he told me so. Instead, we make plans for him to come home in October, just three short months away. I am feeling hopeful for our future, for my future. Patrick and I quickly patch up any holes that are left in our family after my ex-fiancé leaves, spending time together working on school projects, writing letters to Uncle Peter, having family meals with my mother and Ted, and keeping ourselves busy between Sundays.

As I am adjusting to my new routine, Peter is, too. Even though his unit is assigned the responsibility of patrolling one of the most dangerous neighborhoods in Baghdad, he has a relatively safe position working in the arms room. He takes inventory, cleans weaponry, and provides ammunition and assistance to the soldiers who stop by the arms room before and after each patrol. From the bunker, he also spends a good deal of time running communications, monitoring radio channels, and checking in with different teams to make sure that everything is okay. His trademark sense of humor brings some levity to the heavy radio static and reports of gunfire: Other soldiers look forward to hearing his voice crackling over the line, making jokes and silly voices, keeping the troops company from afar.

I let his tales of the routine on base lull me into feeling better about his chances over there. Sometimes, a nagging worry peeks out from underneath his calm facade, and I know that he is probably trying to protect me from the reality of the situation by not fully opening up about what's going on. I also know that his sense of duty drives him to step outside the boundaries of the arms room and into the field, taking over for other men in his unit when they are tired, sick, or go on leave to see their families. He is always the first to volunteer to go out on patrol to replace a soldier who needs help—it is as if he is still trying to make up for his friends who lost their lives in those first surges long ago, well before he ever set foot on Iraqi soil. This is his team, his family now, and he will never let them down again.

After some prying on my part, he tells me what life is like on patrol. During the early days of the war, the infighting between warring factions within Iraq had caused most of the damage in the neighborhoods of Baghdad. He tells me that the worst patrol you can get is the first one in the morning, because most of your work is picking up dead bodies from the fighting the night before. Apart from collecting the collateral damage and disposing of the remains, soldiers on patrol would have to go deep into the neighborhoods, knocking on doors and checking houses for explosive materials, weapons, and insurgents who wished to do the soldiers and the Iraqi people harm.

Back home, a lot of people seem to think it's cut and dried. Much vitriol is spewed on the nightly news by some pundits who would have you believe that the world is one way and one way only—us against them. In Baghdad, the reality is not so clear-cut. Or rather, just different. There, on the front lines, Peter knows that there are bad guys lurking in the dark, in living rooms and cafés and caves alike. But he also knows that there are—and these are the majority, he says— good people, decent people, kind people who are simply unfortunate and caught in the crossfire. He forms close relationships with his interpreters out in the field. On patrol, there are no distinctions, no boundaries; he may be wearing a uniform, and they may speak a language entirely different from our own, but they are there for the same purpose: to protect civilians, to help them find freedom.

Although it isn't necessarily in his mission, Peter can't help but let his compassion flow over onto the people in the neighborhoods he patrols. He becomes attached to them—the interpreters, the families, and the children, especially. While it's not always easy to tell who is a friend and who may be an enemy, he knows that, in the case of these young girls and boys, they are innocent. Just starting out in the world, they have had the misfortune to be born into circumstances so unlike anything Peter and I experienced growing up. While we had our share of heartache, it's nothing compared to the extreme poverty and hopelessness that runs rampant in the neighborhoods of Baghdad. It breaks his heart to see the kids barefoot in the street, limbs lost from explosions, and malnourished. But their spirits still soar, and he loves this about them.

As he's knocking on doors on his patrols, he finds that they often don't have electricity or running water, much less toys to play with. There are some things, he thinks, that he can help fix for them. So he starts to tell me more about them when we talk on the phone. If I'm going to send him things, he says, please don't send him anything, send them things. I look over my shoulder at Patrick, coloring at the kitchen table, waiting for his turn to talk to his uncle, and I know that I have to help Peter help these kids.

"What can I do?" I ask. It dawns on me that I

haven't the faintest idea what they would need. And even if I did, how could I give it to them?

Peter explains that the reality of the situation is dire, and nothing that we could send in a package can fix that. But we can help them have moments of normalcy. I start to think about what that looks like to me, what things put a smile on my own son's face. Candy, toys, games. Crayons, pencils, notebooks. All things, all small things, but things that are much more than the sum of their parts.

"If you're going to send candy," Peter warns, "make sure there's no chocolate. Nothing that can melt."

With my marching orders, Patrick and I start going to stores and filling up big boxes full of soccer balls, coloring books, school supplies. I can see Peter's spirit working through Patrick as I notice the zeal with which he fills up shopping carts for other people, people he will never see or speak to. I am so proud of my son that for a moment it almost alleviates the pain that I feel for the children of Iraq, caught in the middle of something much larger than them, forever a part of something they want no part in. We talk to Patrick's school about organizing a clothing and toy drive for the Iraqi children, and make plans to have Peter collect the items when he's home on leave.

Doing all of this fills me with a sense of purpose that helps the time pass a little faster. It makes me feel less helpless, even though the gestures are undeniably small in the face of all that is going on. The truth is, it helps me feel like I have control over something in my life, a small piece of sanity in the crazy fog of war. I am so far removed from the soldiers, from the senators, from the decision-makers and the bomb-makers. But I can buy a soccer ball. I can send candy.

The patrols have a profound impact on Peter, as the helplessness he feels is like mine multiplied tenfold, coming face-to-face with some of the horrors of the war that he can't fix for its victims. Although the patrols are crucial for security purposes, Peter never misses a chance to turn each visit into a helpful moment for the families inside the crowded, modest village homes. One day, he comes across a young girl who couldn't have been more than four years old. The right part of her upper thigh is critically wounded, and underneath all the blood and gore Peter can see a seething infection that, if left unchecked, will surely kill her in a matter of days. Concerned, he tries not to alarm the girl and her parents too much as he hurriedly asks the interpreters to explain what happened to her.

The interpreters explain to Peter that she was injured from shrapnel from an IED that went off nearby. Her parents are afraid to take her anywhere. They know that staying inside their home means probable death for their child, but what is outside is more uncertain, more daunting. Even if they could safely make it out of Baghdad, they have no money or means to find adequate medical care for her. Peter watches the girl writhing in pain, trying to understand what is happening to her. Though the wound is not fresh, it still bleeds. He knows he must do something.

It takes a lot of convincing on Peter's part, but he is able, with the help of the interpreters, to talk the father into letting his wife and child go with Peter back to his base. It's not an easy task; the man has no reason to trust Peter, and it's likely that he associates the American soldiers with the trouble that has befallen his family. But eventually, he decides that it's the best course of action and gives his blessing. Peter takes the child in his arms and leads the mother to their vehicle and then back to the base, where the medics get to work. The damage is too much for them to help there, they tell Peter, so they take the mother and her daughter to another camp farther away for treatment. Eventually, she makes it home safe—and against all odds, alive.

When Peter tells me this story, I'm not surprised. I know that he would move heaven and earth to stop someone's suffering if he could. But wondering who's looking after him makes my heart ache; it's overwhelming to know that he's so far out of my reach that I can't take care of him. One day over the summer, I get a call from Peter. He sounds worn down and bone-tired, the kind of exhaustion you can really hear over a phone, even from thousands of miles away. I want to know if there's anything I can do. Given how stoic he usually is, protecting me from his needs and wants, I am surprised when the answer comes quickly and easily: "Send fans."

"Fans?" I'm thinking of little Southern belles with ornately stenciled paper fans, trying to keep themselves from sweating off their makeup masks.

"It's hot as hell here," he says, the phrase taking on its full meaning for the first time as it rings in my ears. I think of him sweating through his body armor.

Fans, I write down on a note pad next to the phone, my head dancing with visions of all of the cooling, oscillating contraptions I can fit in my car. I think of the fan aisle at Target and how great it will feel to be able to buy all of those up, package them and bring them down to the post office. I think of making my brother a little more comfortable the only way I can.

"Here's the thing, they need to be battery operated. We can't really get electricity here."

My face sets into a frown, and I know I'll have to change my plans somewhat, but even after scaling them down, I know that I can still do something to help Peter and the men in his unit. Even inside a moving tank or the barracks, the machinery and gear hike up the desert temperatures to an inconceivable 160-degree fireball, so any bit of circulation helps. I go out and buy all the fans I can find, big fans, medium fans, small handheld fans for the soldiers to put inside their tanks and Humvees. I think about the pictures he e-mails me during the week, how flushed his face looks. It's not a piña colada on a balmy beach, but even these tiny fans will help, I know.

It takes a few weeks for mail to reach the base in Baghdad, but when it does, I get the best kind of confirmation from Peter: When he calls that Sunday, he sounds lively, thankful, and happy to have something as simple as a small, battery powered fan to help him get through those long desert days and nights. And I am more than happy.

Something starts to shift inside Peter, I know. In his last letter home, dated July 2, he admits to my father that he is afraid. I know he would never say as much to me, because he doesn't want me to be more scared than I already am, but in addition to the regular complaints about camel spiders, sandstorms, and homesickness, he has told my father he's not sure he's going to make it out of there. That every time he goes out on patrol, it might be the last time he comes back on his own two feet. Every breath might very well be his last.

His next call, which comes four days later, is not so uplifting as when we spoke about the fans. He calls to say that something horrible has happened, and I can feel my heart catch in my throat. He's speaking to me himself, though, I remind myself, so it can't be so bad.

It can't be him. He is not dead. I catch myself checking just to make sure it's him on the line. I convince myself that I recognize his voice, and my ears open again to take in the information he is trying to give me.

In all his time in the Army, I've never heard him sound like this. The sound is unmistakable: Peter is crying. I've heard him cry about everything from hurting himself playing in the woods when we were kids to heartbreak at the hands of a woman, but never once have I heard him cry over the phone about the war and its consequences.

He can't bring himself to say the words at first. "You're going to need to send more fans," he tells me, before bursting into tears. "The Bradley blew up. Some of the fans were in there."

But his tears tell a different story. Finally, he tells me that two of his best friends have been killed while out on patrol, and, much like the first time he had to accept news like this, he can't seem to shake the feeling that it should have been him.

Trained as a sniper, Peter sits up in the turret on top of the tank on patrol. He has had some close calls—almost catching on fire once when low-hanging electrical cables, sagging from so many people stealing electricity from the main breakers, caught on the turret. But for the most part, he doesn't tell us about these things. No matter how dangerous things get, that doesn't stop him. He always volunteers himself because he feels like he has no children of his own, no wife to come home to. If anyone should take a bullet, he thinks, it should be him. So it's not unusual when, covering for a friend, he takes a shift one afternoon on patrol. The next shift—in the same tank—an IED hit the patrol, and his friends were killed.

For Peter, this is almost too much to take. Each time he takes over a patrol for his fellow soldiers, he feels as if there's some kind of angel or spirit pushing him there—that everything happens for a reason, and he might be able to save his brothers in arms from leaving widows and orphans back home. If something were going to happen, he thought, it should happen to him. To know that his friends were killed in the very same tank that he was manning only hours before crushes him—it is no good telling him that it wasn't his fault or that there wasn't anything he could have done to prevent it.

It is the only time he ever opens up to me about being truly afraid. When he comes home on leave in October, he doesn't bring it up again, but I can see the maimed bodies haunting him, ghosts loosed from their bodies and making a home in his eyes.

FIVE

Home on Leave

It's October of 2007, the month that I should have been running around preparing for my wedding. Though many people would have the desire to hide in a hole and never come out—particularly during the same month that they should have been walking down the aisle—I couldn't care less. I am too busy preparing for a different kind of milestone: Peter's first leave home since he began his tour in Iraq.

Knowing that Peter will be home soon is the most thrilling feeling in the world. Without any other military families to turn to for support, our family has been feeling undeniably lost. Although it's hard for us to sort through our feelings, much less talk about them, we try to support each other in all the little ways, all the small gestures that show our love for one another. All three adults are employed full-time, but when we're not working, we try to spend time together and help Patrick move through his childhood in relative normalcy. My father will easily pick up on when I'm stressed or overwhelmed, and will find something to distract me, taking me out for meals or to the firing range to blow off some steam. He takes Patrick to the Yacht Club where Peter, Ted, and I learned how to sail in our summers off, finding some peace out on the water. My mother helps me with Patrick, too, taking part in our day-to-day life, going for walks up to the playground or taking Patrick to the pool or for a bike ride. And always, at the end of the day, no matter how busy we are, we will sit down together for dinner as a family.

But there is profound loneliness, a separation from the world. Our friends and extended family know that Peter is in Iraq and have some idea of the seriousness of what we're going through, but as compassionate as they are, the true feeling of being understood escapes us. No one can know what we're going through unless they go through it themselves.

So when Peter touches down at the airport and I can finally hold him, it feels like it's the first time that I can exhale in a long, long time. All the mixed emotions I've been holding in over these long months come flooding out. The time spent guessing how he was doing and if he were getting enough sleep, enough water, enough food—if he were safe, if he were injured—has weighed on our family in ways that we haven't begun to comprehend. The feeling of relief that I experience upon being able to hug him and talk to him face-to-face is overwhelming. I almost feel as if I can't really stand up, and have to take my time moving from chair to chair just in case my legs fall out from under me. I make sure there is always a wall or seat nearby in case I faint. After the birth of Patrick, seeing Peter come out of that plane was the best moment of my life. I look at him like he's an angel, like something I dreamed up. But it's really happening, it's true: My brother is safe, he is alive, and he is finally home.

The next three weeks are truly blissful. Not a second goes by that I don't thank all my lucky stars and whatever is watching over us for the opportunity to spend this time together. Our family is finally able to sleep at night without crying ourselves there; we can finally sit and enjoy a nice meal together without that ever-present tension in our shoulders. The knot in my stomach is gone, dissipated with my worry. It's almost as if the past months have been a very bad dream. I try not to think about how quickly these weeks will fly by. For now, having Peter here is all that matters to me.

There are many celebrations, toasts, and moments dedicated to commemorating the occasion, but what Peter enjoys most are the little things. Even though he has only been in Iraq a few months, the world that Peter has known day in and day out couldn't have been further from what he was used to at home. So being able to go to his favorite restaurant or sitting and watching a movie with Patrick is an indescribable lifeline. Even though I can see that he is haunted by the ghosts of war, his face sometimes takes on a lightness that I haven't seen since we were kids. He spends every minute he can with Patrick—going to his lacrosse games, cheering him on, letting him know he is loved. He goes to Patrick's school and leads his fourth-grade class in the Pledge of Allegiance, then stays for hours to answer the kids' many questions. With the uncanny, often unintentional, maturity that sometimes comes with youth, they don't shy away from asking him the hard questions. One boy wants to know why, if he knew he would have to go to war, he would even join the Army in the first place. His answer, simple and truthful: "So you guys will never have to."

After he leaves, they take up a collection of toys, candy, and books to send to the schoolchildren of Iraq. He and I go out to see his best friend Evan's band play at a bar, and everyone downs drinks and swaps stories like no time has gone by at all.

Not all of the changes that have overtaken him are bad ones. He is more patient, more appreciative of the little things. More than once, he stops to smell the fresh morning air or to stand in a cool rain shower. The fall foliage blazes for him differently than it does for me; he truly knows what it means to be in the presence of a natural miracle that we all take for granted, simply because he's been faced with the very possible reality of not being there for anything at all. "God, the grass is green," he says to me one day as I am driving us on an errand. I watch him shake his head in amazement and, while I can't fully appreciate the moment the way he can, I know that it's important.

But there are times at night when all the green grass and all the starry skies can't erase what he's seen. He has a thousand-yard stare, and I catch him looking off into the distance sometimes, contemplating things that I would never be able to understand. I know that he's not the same Peter I used to know: He has seen things, horrible things that he'll never be able to unsee. He'll never be able to process them with me. He'll never be able to shed the weight that his soul has taken on out there in the desert. Every night, he sits in front of the television for hours, long after the rest of us have given up and gone to bed. He looks at his watch, checking on what time it is in Baghdad, thinking about what his fellow soldiers are up to. He watches the news for hints of activity, obsessing about where and when the blurry bombs onscreen were going off. I know that he wants to be here with us, but I know that he's also torn—he has another family now, too, and they are far, far away from Michigan.

★ ★ ★

The weekend that I was to be married, we drive up to our family's cabin on Michigan's Upper Peninsula. Built by Grandpa Neesley, it's a simple cabin outside a little city called Rapid River. I always love going to the cabin—not only does it mean that I'm going to get to spend wonderful time with some of my best friends in the world—my family—but going there is like crossing into another universe.

The way up from Grosse Pointe is a typical expressway drive: exits every other mile, the same stuff at the same truck stops, the same McDonald's, the same scenery. But at some point, you cross over the gold-lit Mackinac Bridge, and all of the sudden a beautiful, untamed wilderness unfolds before you. And it's never more beautiful than it is in the fall. The leaves are changing colors, the air is clear, and the nights are just starting to turn cold enough to drive out the throngs of summer tourists. Getting off the highway, you drive and wind through tiny towns that have three or so simple foursquare houses, a gas station, a grocery store, and sometimes a local watering hole. There's not a chain restaurant in sight, and it's the best that small-town America has to offer, combined with the majesty of the open wilds.

When we drive past Lake Michigan, in the blue-black water I can see the reflection of the foliage, looking like it's on fire. The air smells clean, and even though it's cold, I roll my window down to take it in.

In less than a month, the entire area will be blanketed with suffocating snow, but right now, this moment feels perfect.

I know that I should be sad about my wedding, but having Peter here makes that feel small. I try not to sweat the small stuff when he's around, so that I can savor every moment. With Peter home, it's even easier to see how important it is not to settle for something less than I deserve—we only have one life, and we have to make the most of it. My relationship wasn't going to help me live the best life that I could, and I understand that now more than ever, with Peter by my side to give me strength.

We get to the cabin, and Patrick and Peter tumble out of the car and chase each other around outside while my father and I bring in the supplies for our stay. Everything is just as we left it the last time: the bunk beds, the wool blankets, the simple furniture, the wood-burning stove that we would crowd around for warmth at night. I feel safe and like a child again, and the world seems simpler, more comprehensible than it has in a long time.

I can tell that it's a healing time for Peter, too. He loves it up here; our little cabin has always been his favorite place. He loves the woods, in particular—growing up, he always thought it was funny to scare everyone once the sun had set and the fire was roaring inside, by creeping around in the woods at night.

While the rest of us are a little skittish about the un-familiar sounds of the dark woods, Peter loves them. At night, long after the rest of us have gone to bed, he still sits up—but instead of gazing at never-ending footage of a war zone, he gazes up at the stars. It seems like there are millions and billions of stars, new stars, undiscovered stars, stars that you can never see in the city because of all of the lights. He stays up and stares at falling stars and the Milky Way for hours in the cold. I can rest easy up here, too, because I know he's been brought some small comfort from those tiny burning lights. I fall asleep, dead to the world, in my bottom bunk, and don't wake up when he climbs in at the close of the wee hours to take his space on the top bunk, just like when we were little kids.

Our last night there, I am a little quieter than usual. I know that the visit is coming to a close, and I'm not looking forward to facing the sadness that waits for us when we leave. Peter suggests that we go for a walk. I try to get Patrick to come, but he shakes his head; he's too afraid that Uncle Peter is going to jump out from behind a tree and scare him half to death. Peter says goodnight to Patrick, and we load up our pockets with beer and butterscotch schnapps—a camp tradition—and make our way out into the woods.

I don't even have to ask where we're heading; I know as soon as we set out that we're going to Peter's favorite spot. A quarter of a mile out from the cabin, there's a clearing where the woods open up into a beautiful field. On one side of the clearing, there's a hill that you can lie on and gaze up at the stars and down at the valley at the same time. It's the most beautiful place in the world—and so peaceful. Peter and I know that spending time here will be good to soothe our souls, which have already started to form calluses around all the fear and anxiety that comes from the unknown.

We sit there, leaning up against each other, for hours, just drinking and talking. I open up to him more about what happened with my relationship and why it fell apart and admitted that Peter had been right, that my fiancé didn't care deeply enough for Patrick and me and couldn't offer us what we needed. He listens and gives me hugs when I need them.

He reassures me that the future needn't look as bleak as the recent past has led us to believe. He promises that when he gets home from this tour in Iraq he will try to get stationed in Michigan for a while in order to spend some time at home with us. He says he wants to work as a recruiting officer and buy himself a little time stateside for at least a few months.

That is music to my ears. I had long ago accepted the fact that Peter had a force much stronger than me driving him to those distant shores. Hearing him say this, I believe that things are really going to be okay—that finally, things are turning around.

We sit, laughing and crying and drinking and making promises, for hours more. We talk about our future, but we talk about our memories, too. About stuff that happened before life got hard for us. And about what life will be like after Iraq, about how he will make sure that Patrick is raised right, that he'll always be there for him. I feel at ease and safer with every promise.

It comes back to me in letters and e-mails and the news that war zones are called theaters, stages. It strikes me then how much it sounds like it's all a bad dream, a horrific play—one where, at the end when the curtains come down and the lights go up, even dead soldiers will rise again, live to fight another day, to kiss their wives and sisters and children and stand in their front lawns in summertime like the rest of us.

Eventually, we make it back to the cabin, drunkenly creeping in, trying not to wake Patrick and my dad. I slide into the bottom bunk, and he clamors up to the top. It is the first time since we were children that we've been in the bunk beds like this, and we're both acting just as playful and innocent as we were then. He goofs around with me, dropping things on me from above and pretending like they are spiders. It's playful, sweet, and reminiscent of our early days. Our worries were left out in that field.

We head back home the next day, and then the night comes: the night before Peter has to go back. We all have dinner together, laughing and enjoying every moment. We take pictures. I iron his uniform with care, the one he will wear on the long plane ride back to Iraq. We try to hold ourselves together, but the fear that lies underneath is palpable. At the end of the night, Peter takes Patrick by the shoulders, kisses him, and says, "I love you, little buddy. Take care of your mom for me until I come home."

I drive Peter over to our father's house, where he will spend his last night before Dad takes him to the airport the next morning. A cold rain falls around us, and Peter looks out the window, saying how much he'll miss this weather. I try one last time to convince him to stay, offering to move us all to another country, one where we wouldn't be at war, and where no one would declare war on us. But I know it's futile; he's leaving us again.

When we pull up to our father's house in Detroit, I get out of the car with him, and we say our good-byes on the street. He holds me as I let my tears fall. I make him promise that he will come home safe to us, and I tell him again how much we love him and need him. I remember to add how proud I am of him. He promises me that he will come home. We stand in the rain until our hair is soaking wet, our clothes damp and cold, reassuring each other that this isn't good-bye. We promise phone calls, packages, e-mails, and letters. He gives me one last hug, one last smile, one last "I love you, babe." Then, I force myself away.

After I make it off the block, I am sobbing so violently that I have to pull over. I can't breathe. I can't see. My heart is pounding and aching with a pain that I know, even then, I'll never find the words to express.

As I try to pull myself together, I think of his promises. I carry these with me when I wake up the next morning, thinking of his plane taking off into the blue, and I start to feel a little better. After all those months of worrying, I'm finally feeling like life is not so unmanageable, like maybe the future could be good. Even great. This time, when we see him off at the airport, I feel safer, less alone, less scared. It seems like Peter knows he's going to be okay, and that makes me feel like it's not just a possibility, but a certain truth.

SIX

Mama and Boris

Here in Michigan, it looks like it's going to be a mild winter, one that we will spend wishing for snow. Because I want to protect him from whatever cold and wet might come his way, I still spend time in the morning getting Patrick bundled up in his winter gear, always to much protestation from the small, muffled boy inside the layers. After I see him off to school, I daydream about what life was like for me when I was his age, spending hours out in the fields with Peter making snowmen and snow angels, sledding until our hands were raw and our noses red. Growing up seems to make the winter less joyful, more inconvenient, and I take a moment to offer up gratitude to whoever is watching over us that I can still appreciate the seasons, unlike the troops who melt away, much like our snowmen did, in Iraq.

I pray more, now, something I've never done before. It's all part of something I find myself working

toward, some kind of accumulation of good karma in the universe. I go above and beyond with random acts of kindness—donating blood, donating clothes, donating money I don't have. I do anything I can think of to try to convince the universe to grant us an acceptable outcome, to return Peter home to us. Deep down I know I don't have any say in the matter, but equally deep down, I hope that I might. I pray that I might.

Not long after Peter returns to Iraq, our beautiful night in the woods receded into memory, we start getting some happy news from the field. In these calls, Peter sounds more like his old self and less like the anxious, sometimes hollow man that I've seen him grow into during the war. He'd like to think that I don't notice the change, that he's protected me from it, but he is my twin in spirit—the strings that pull at his heart wrap themselves around mine, too. It turns out that Peter has found some unlikely companions in the middle of the war zone, which reminds all of us that the world can still be a little bit wonderful even in the most complicated times.

Growing up, we always had animals. Starting with Casey and Arrow, our keepers in the woods, our family would keep cats and dogs. We both loved them, but it was Peter who seemed to communicate with the animals on a deeper level than anyone else we knew. He was drawn to their innocence, and their pure emotions. Arrow, the rusty-colored springer spaniel, was Peter's

Once my care package is off, I start decorating the house with Patrick. We put twinkling lights outside, running them along the bushes and over the doorway. We bring home a Christmas tree for the living room, and we all decorate it together, each putting on our favorite ornaments that we carefully unwrap from layers of boxes and decades-old tissue paper. Each night, by the fire, I watch all the classic holiday cartoons with Patrick—something that Peter would usually do with him. We go to the mall to see Santa, or one of Santa's helpers, as I explain to Patrick.

One night, the whole family piles into the car, and we go take the drive down Lakeshore Drive, which stretches along Lake St. Clair in Grosse Pointe. There, huge mansions built in better times by industrial giants like Henry Ford and other well-to-do Michigan families line the waterfront. For our family and many others, it becomes a Christmas tradition to drive down the road at night, slowing the car to a crawl and ogling the holiday decorations—the thousands of starry light bulbs, the statuettes of reindeer, the manger, the elves, and everything in between. Patrick and I press our faces against the car windows, and our breath fogs up the glass, leaving clownish impressions against the night sky.

Still, even with all the holiday cheer, it doesn't quite feel like Christmas to me. Without Peter there, it's just not the same. I'm sad and happy all at once when a call comes at the usual time on December 23—it's Peter, and I am sitting in the kitchen listening to his voice coming my way from another world. It's a wonderful present to get to speak to him, but like the feeling I get when I think of my Grandpa Bohn on Christmas, it leaves me hollow and haunted all the same.

I ask Peter how he is, but he's concerned with other things. He's worried because his package for Patrick hasn't arrived at the house yet. I roll my eyes over on my end of the line and tell him not to worry. "Are you kidding? This is the last thing you need to be stressing about," I say, really meaning it. Patrick will understand if his Uncle Peter's present gets delayed in the mail, or even if he hadn't gotten him a present at all.

"It's just important to me," Peter says, exasperated.

I say a silent prayer that the doorbell will ring with the present while we're on the line, just so that I can give Peter the satisfaction of knowing that it got here in time for Christmas. My prayers unanswered, I consider lying for a moment, and then think the better of it. "It will be fine," I reassure him, again, really meaning it. "It's not going to be the same without you," I say, choking back tears, and he immediately tries to cheer me up.

"Your package is here," he says, the devilish note in his voice hinting that he plans to tear into it at any moment.

I sniffle, regain my composure. "You'd better not open it until Christmas."

"I promise."

I believe him; I know that his word is his bond. Which is why it crushes me a little to hear him say that he has some news for me—he is going to re-enlist in January. I hear how happy he sounds as he gives me the news, and I somehow have the composure not to scream into the phone or burst into tears. The Army has given Peter the direction and the drive that he's been searching for all his life, I think. I can't take that away from him. I have to be happy for him. I grit my teeth and thank him for telling me, asking him a few questions about where the next swearing in will happen and when. Somewhere in my battered heart I'm a little angry—has he already forgotten all the promises we'd made up at the woods?

"It's going to happen over here," he says.

I am quiet.

"It's going to be great, Care. I'm doing what I was meant to do. I'm really making a difference."

I wonder if he knows what a difference he always made to me, to Patrick. He never felt that he was good enough, but I know better. "That's great, Peter. I'm happy for you," I say—this time, not really meaning it.

Here is the truth: While I may not have been happy for him, I was brimming with pride. My heart was heavy with the thought that this would be the next fifteen years or so of my life—holding my breath for months of deployment, stealing hugs at the airport when I could, and dreading the knock that could come at our door any day. But I know that this is part of loving a soldier, and I couldn't be more proud of my big little brother.

We wrap up our conversation as Patrick starts clanging around in the kitchen in his pajamas, getting ready for a cozy snow day in front of the television.

"Don't you open that present, Peter Collins Neesley," I tell him once more.

"I won't."

"Wait for Christmas."

"I will."

He promises to call us on Christmas, we say our good-byes, and I hang up the phone.

EIGHT

The Department of the Army Regrets to Inform You . . .

I wake up on Christmas morning to a rhythmic thumping that shakes my mattress. As my eyes adjust to the dawn streaming through the blinds, I see my son's curls bouncing up and down as he jumps on the bed. I groan and swivel around to look at the alarm clock.

"Patrick, please. . . ." I start, pleading for just five more minutes of rest.

Patrick, a tough negotiator, laughs and shakes his head. He's so excited to go downstairs and see what Santa has left him. I take a deep breath and try to remember what it's like to have such unfettered joy. It's on this memory that I'm able to drag myself out of bed and join Patrick, trying to keep him from racing too loudly down the stairs, lest he wake Ted and my mother.

The sun has yet to fully come up. I flip on the Christmas lights and start the fire, quieting Patrick down by giving him his stocking to open up on the couch. I go into the kitchen to get coffee and breakfast going, and pop open a bottle of champagne—we always have mimosas on Christmas morning, and if I have to be up at 6:30 A.M., I think, I deserve a little champagne.

I can hear Patrick's muffled pleasure from the den, uncovering the small things I've left for him in his stocking. Candy and pocket games are appetizers for him until he gets to tear into the big presents glittering in the colored lights of the tree. The fire licks and crackles at the wood as it really gets going, warming the whole house. After I pop the cork on the champagne bottle, I think I hear a knock, but then think the better of it. It's too early for that; it must have just been an echo against the kitchen tiles.

There it is again, though, purposeful and unmistakable: three quick raps on the door. I look at the clock—just past 7:00 A.M.—and roll my eyes. It never crosses my mind that it's anyone other than Luke, Patrick's playmate across the street, who has undoubtedly also gotten his parents up way too early and is now coming over here to compare Christmas loot. "Patrick, please tell Luke it's too early right now. You'll come over after we open presents and have family time," I say, pouring the orange juice into a pitcher.

I hear Patrick tumble off the couch and pad over to the door, but when I don't hear the door open, I stick my head out of the kitchen to see what's going on. "I don't know who that is," he says, pointing at the door.

The large window in front of the door has a sheer curtain blocking the view, but I can make out the shadows of two grown men outside—not Luke from across the street. One of the figures is wearing a flattened crown that tapers down in the front—my blood runs cold as I recognize the shape as an army hat. My thoughts are racing a thousand miles a minute. On a normal day, my heart would have skipped a beat when I heard the knock the first time, but something about today felt safe, sacred. My voice cracks as I tell Patrick to go into the living room and sit down.

It sounds like a jet engine is roaring in my ears, drowning out the sound of my own breath. Or maybe I'm not breathing. The figures on the other side of the door can see me, but I will not open the door for them, not even a crack—I lean against the wall, my back against it, my head bent against the cold, hard molding around the door. There come muffled pleas for me to open the door, politely tempered with standard military issued Ma'ams. I feel warm tears flowing down my face and fall to my lips, which are numb with shock and fear. I try to rationalize what's happening—tell myself that Peter is just hurt. That he's coming home with a broken leg or a bruised ribcage.

I almost float above myself, hearing mumbled whispers passing through my lips—go away, go away, please go away. You have to go away. I'm not opening the door. Please stop. Please go away.

But the men do not go away. Their knocks grow louder, their voices more demanding. "Please, ma'am. Please open the door for us. We have to tell you something."

I open the door just a crack and steady my body against it so that they cannot push into our home. "You have to go away," I say.

"Ma'am, we have to speak with you. Please let us in."

My voice sounds as though it's a stranger's. "Go away," I say again, louder this time, my voice cracking.

I feel something taking over my arms, taking over my body. It's not just my voice now that belongs to someone else. My hands, as they wrap around the doorknob, are not mine. My face, shocked awake by the cold air that rushes through the door, is not mine. I don't know why I open the door. But I've done it. They come inside.

"The Department of the Army regrets to inform you . . ." they begin.

The words echo around in my skull. The world is spinning. I hear what they say as I'll hear nothing else in my lifetime, but at the same time, I can't believe that it's what I've heard. "The Department of the Army regrets to inform you that your soldier, Sergeant Peter C. Neesley, died in his sleep this morning in Baghdad."

They give me a minute to take this in, but there are not enough minutes, not enough hours. Then, they begin to ask if anyone else is home, if my mother is here. They want to speak to her. I put my hand up and quietly shut the door. I turn around, the ground shaking underneath me like a fault line has opened up underneath our house, like at any moment I will fall off the precipice into my personal hell. I see that Patrick is standing there; he's tiptoed in so quietly that I didn't hear him behind me, and it is obvious that he's heard the whole thing. His eyes are huge and full of tears, and the innocence that was in them only moments ago seems to be lost now forever.

I go to him, and I put my arms around him and then I fall to the ground on my knees. From deep inside me comes a wail—a horrible sound—that rumbles out of me from somewhere inside that I didn't know existed. It's a horrible sound that spins out from a web of horrible pain that glues me to the ground. Ted and my mother run down the stairs, awakened by my screams.

I can't even tell them what has just happened, but

it doesn't take them long to figure it out. Nothing connects for me; I try again and again to wrap my mind around the news. I had just talked to Peter the other day. He was perfectly fine, perfectly healthy. And he died in his sleep on Christmas morning. The men behind the door can give us no further answers—they will conduct an investigation, but we may not find out the results for quite some time. They report that a casualty assistance officer will come to visit with us later. They offer to sit by our side and pray with us and help us make phone calls to whomever we need to call. Our response is unanimous, echoing my earlier pleas: We want them to go away.

We all go into the living room, surrendering to the state of shock. The world has cracked wide open— there was the before, when we had Peter, and the after, which would be everything else. We look at each other in silence, all trying to come to grips with whatever it is that we are supposed to do next.

I pick up the phone and call my father, because while my mother is too hysterical to make the call, I am floating in a cocoon of numbness that allows me to speak and move. I'm not sure how long it will last, and I want to dial his number and have this conversation as fast as I can before the next wave of sobbing hits. It turns out that the Army has already been to his house, and he didn't call us because he thought it would be better coming from the representatives—not to mention he was too shocked to pick up the phone. It's not long before we start to get phone calls from the newspapers and television stations that want to speak to us about our loss. Just hours before we had no idea what the day would hold for us, and to have the media already contacting us feels horribly disrespectful, rude, and wrong. Needless to say, we have no comment for them.

We decide to call our extended family and some of Peter's closest friends because we know that tomorrow morning the news will be printed in the paper with or without our comments. I take on the task of calling my mother's family, while my father calls his own family. I call each of my aunts, one by one. Then, when I can take it no longer, I call Peter's best friend, Evan, to tell him that he will have to take over the chain of phone calls, because I can't handle any more calls. The words from the Army representatives ring out in my head over and over as I am forced to relive receiving the horrible news: the Department of the Army regrets to inform you . . .

My mother goes up to her room, shuts the door, gets in bed, and refuses to come out. Friends and family want to come and offer their support, and it all falls into my lap to take care of the people who want to be around us, who are trying to come to grips with

Peter's death. But I am in no state to help them heal. I still have not truly processed what has happened, and no matter how much people offer to help or give me whatever I need, I have no idea what I need. Or, I do know, it's just something that no one can give me, something that I will never have again: I need my brother.

NINE

A Hero
Returns Home

The days since Peter left us have passed in a clouded nightmare-scape, all rendered alike in bleakness and sorrow. There are phone calls to be made, people to speak to. Two separate casualty assistance officers are assigned to our family. The tragedy seems to be taking place split over two houses: My mother and father have not recovered from the bitterness of their divorce, and although they wish each other no harm, they are not on speaking terms. This leaves me as an exhausted go-between during all of the decision-making and preparations. Peter's life, and death, have morphed into a list of tasks to check off and accomplish, all bringing us not nearer to him, it seems, but farther away. And even though I am mired in mourning this whole time, I am cognizant of how much reckoning is yet to come when things finally sink in.

We receive word from the Army that Peter's body will come home to us on New Year's Eve. Arrangements have been made to bring him in the cargo hold of a commercial airliner, and we are to go to the airport, accompanied by police escorts and two separate limousines to carry us, to claim him. Later, I would find out that it was an option to have him flown in on a private army plane—something I would have leapt at the chance for. That option gets lost in the shuffle, though, and I try my best to become at ease with the fact that hundreds of strangers will be accompanying Peter on this last journey.

Our immediate family, some of our extended family, and two of Peter's best friends, Evan and Scott, all meet and break off into two groups, taking seats in the limos and embarking on the cold, quiet ride to the airport. Rain pelts the tinted windows, glazing the already somber moment with more darkness. It feels as though all the light has been squeezed out of me and is now lost up there in the atmosphere with Peter. At this moment, I don't feel as though it will ever return.

The half-hour drive to the airport stretches out in silence. Either no one knows what to say or isn't willing to say it. In our limo, the dull heat from the bodies of my mother, Evan, Scott, my mother's relatives, Patrick, and me is the only hint that there is even life here. Out of nowhere and apropos of nothing, the window fogs up in front of Evan and nowhere else, the condensation pattern coming into focus as a single, legible, unambiguous word: "FUCK."

Evan grabs my hand, his whispers breaking the silence of the ride. "Did you see that?" he asks.

I dig into Evan's hand with my own cold fingers and nod. "That's Peter," I said.

The moment passes as quickly as it came, and the obscenity fades from view. Peter's favorite word, there in an instant and gone in a flash. I know there are a thousand reasons, most of them rooted in reality, why that word could be etched into the window. But the fact that out of all the grimy graffiti that could have popped up on the windows, that particular word popped up at that particular moment in front of that particular person—the coincidences are too uncanny to ignore. I close my eyes and take in the moment, the first of many when Peter will communicate with me. I say a silent prayer to him and thank him for the comfort that this one lighthearted moment brings to us. That one syllable, tossed off now into the ether, has opened a small window in our hearts and, for the moment, we can breathe a little easier. I know that we will need that breathing room for what comes next.

We pull into the airport, and we are escorted directly to the tarmac. The plane we are waiting for hasn't arrived yet, so we all continue to huddle in the limos until the last minute, when we will stand out in the cold rain to welcome Peter home in the only way we're able to now. Waiting for us at the gate is a straight-backed honor guard standing as taciturn witness to an all too familiar sight. Above us, we hear the thunder of an incoming plane, and as the bulbous nose of the passenger jet crawls into view, we steel ourselves for the damp and cold and get out.

I am not prepared for the sight that greets me when I look up into the windows of the airport terminal. Standing there, curious and watchful, are swarms of passengers—some waiting for takeoff, some recently landed, but all peering through the windows at our family. Though I'm sure they are trying to be respectful, I can't help but resent the feeling it causes me as I'm trying to live out a very painful, very private moment in front of an audience. Just as I do every time a member of the news media calls our house, I feel like part of a freak show, like my unmentionable, unfathomable grief has been put on display for a world of strangers to see.

The belly of the plane opens up. We are told that, inside the plane, the captain is making an announcement to the passengers to please stay in their seats and observe a moment of silence and respect for a passenger none of them had known about—that a hero is coming home. Peter's flag-draped casket is carried from the dark hold under the plane.

The honor guard, a group of eight soldiers dressed in military garb, act as the pallbearers, removing the casket from the plane and placing it into the hearse.

favorite—he even had a stuffed dog named Arrow, for when he couldn't convince the real creature to climb under the covers with him for a suffocating squeeze or two. So when Peter calls and excitedly tells us stories about a small pack of five dogs that has started coming around the base—a mother and her four pups—I laugh and think, of course he has pets in Iraq.

Peter says that one day, he noticed a rustling just outside the walls of the base—a castle that used to belong to Saddam Hussein overlooking the muddy Tigris River. When he went outside to investigate, he saw a dusty troupe of mottled, almost camouflaged, puppies rolling in the sand, all presided over by a serious, sleek, dark presence—their mother. The Army doesn't allow soldiers to keep animals on the base, Peter explains, and he knew that it was dangerous for them to be spotted so near to the walls, as often stray animals will be ordered to be put down if they are found to be engaging with soldiers. I know that Peter would give his life for the Army, but that loyalty isn't going to be strong enough for him to obey this particular rule. I can hear it in his voice.

"What are you going to do?" I ask, worried about Peter getting in trouble just as much as the animals.

"I don't know," he says. "I'll figure something out. I couldn't really get close to them, so I'll have to see if they're there again tomorrow. I'm going to go check as soon as I get a chance."

When Peter went back the next day, the animals were nowhere to be found. It wasn't until he was out on patrol again that he saw them, farther away from the base this time and playing near a road. After a couple more sightings, he says, he figured out this was where they were spending most of their time. He spends a good two weeks feeding the mother dog, trying to gain her trust. Each time, he says, she comes a little closer, trusting him a little more. Meanwhile, the puppies look on from a safe distance—she always stands between them and Peter, making sure that they aren't going to get into any trouble. She looks nothing like them save for the flop of her ears, Peter says, but she must be their mother. Her maternal instinct is in overdrive.

One day, Peter e-mails us a few photos of the dogs, and we can see that he's gained the trust of the mother and is able to sit in the pack while they play around him. Finally, he has made contact. In the pictures, he is smiling while he ruffles the hair of the mother, whom he calls Mama, and the four puppies, who nip at his hands, the dust flying around them as they whip around the camera frame. They're like little balls of fur and energy, and he looks so happy to be in the midst of them. Peter reports that he goes back every day to their spot to play with them, feed them spare scraps from his pre-packaged ready-to-eat meals (MREs) or from the mess, when he can sneak some out, and keep them company.

Much like his calls when he first started befriending and helping the local children, it's clear that Peter has a new mission within his mission: He wants to help these dogs. He hasn't seen anyone around who could be their owner, and a war zone is not the safest or most welcoming place for our four-legged friends, he says. The people there have other things—life-and-death things—on their minds, and rescuing animals just isn't a priority. That's why he needs us to help him by sending him dog food, chew bones, toys, anything that we could find that we'd be able to send over for the dogs.

Once again, I head off to the store for supplies. Patrick is my little helper, grabbing toys and treats off the shelves and flinging them into our cart. I have to remind him that we can't ship everything to Iraq; there's only so much our boxes will hold. We both feel that even though we've never met these dogs, they're ours, too; an extension of our family, someone to keep Peter smiling.

Peter sends us pictures of the dogs playing with our toys, and it's a great feeling. It's the first time they've seen anything like what we take for granted for our pets over here. They eye the brightly colored chew toys like we'd look at gold bars, and I envy how happy they look, how carefree.

Soon, Peter tells us that he can't find two of the puppies. They've wandered off, or worse. My heart sinks, and I hope against hope that they've just found another friendly person to sit with for now, but I know that's unlikely. I don't tell Patrick about my fears, not wanting to burden him with any more sadness. He has already started to come home from school with poems he's written about the costs of war—how it scares him, how it makes him sad. Peter's news about the pups continues to grow darker, shadowed by a cruel reality. One day, he sees one of the pups run into the road and get hit by a car, dying immediately right in front of him. It's then that he decides the spot where they've been hanging out is an unsafe location, and he's determined to make a better place for Mama and the remaining puppy to stay.

He sends us another picture of himself, this time proudly kneeling beside a small doghouse he and some of his friends have built outside the walls of the base. They've painted it in the colors of their unit, and dragged some old bedding inside to make it comfortable. It's small compared to the looming castle in the background, but to the dogs, it's like a castle of their own. He carries Mama and her puppy to the new home, and places them inside, feeding them treats that we've sent to make sure they know this is their new safe place. During the day, they might wander off, but he is pleased to find that they always return.

He sends us another picture of the puppy, a close up, where he's cradling him in his hands. Peter's eyes are clear, happy, and peaceful, looking straight at the camera. The mischievous puppy is in the bottom of the frame, looking like he's about to wriggle off and get into some trouble. Peter says that he's named the puppy Boris, after one of his friends, a fallen soldier. He doesn't say anything more about that.

* * *

At the beginning of December, Peter's voice is strained with worry during one of his Sunday morning calls. Everything is fine with him, but Boris's health seems to be mysteriously failing. It is rare to hear this kind of panic in his voice—he is a seasoned soldier who has seen all kinds of things in the field, but this sick puppy seems to have him undone. I can sense how important the dogs are to him, how much he loves them and how much of a comfort they are to him. It's also, I think, probably the only "normal" thing that he gets to do all day.

"What's wrong with him?" I want to know.

"I don't know. I don't know anything about this!"

I try to keep him calm and think through a solution, like he would always do with me when I was running around overwhelmed and panic-stricken as an outcast teenager. "His hair is falling out and he's scratching. A lot."

Before we hang up, I promise him that I'm going to get to the bottom of it. I call local vets I know and describe the problem, getting lists of questions from them in return to ask Peter. One of the vets gives me medicated soap, which I'm able to send through the mail. No vet could accurately diagnose the problem without seeing the puppy, though; they all point out that, as a street dog, it could be many things—scabies, dry skin from the desert, some other kind of infection. As a parent and a pet owner, I know how frustrating it can be to see a small, helpless thing suffering and be unable to talk to it to find out what is going on. I cross my fingers that the soap works. Peter gets the soap and immediately rushes out to start bathing Boris, sticking him in a small bucket and tending to his sore spots with a washcloth.

Meanwhile, Mama starts trusting Peter more and more, letting him pet her and play with her. Peter teaches Boris how to fetch a tennis ball, although the distracted little furball apparently doesn't take instruction too easily. Even though his team laughs at him when he makes a beeline for the doghouse on all of his breaks, they join him there, too, taking comfort in the companionship of the animals. He e-mails us pictures all the time, and we can see the puppy growing as fast as Patrick is.

Eventually, we start talking about bringing the dogs home with him when his tour ends. We naively hatch a plan that involves me flying to Kuwait and him sneaking them across the border alone in a car borrowed from a sympathetic local friend. Peter probably knows how insane that sounds, but it doesn't stop him. He's worried about what will happen to the dogs when his tour is up; he knows they might be shot or euthanized, or they might wander off and be struck by a car. It isn't a question of if they are coming back; it is just a question of how.

SEVEN

Do Not Open Until Christmas

Since this is our first Christmas without Peter, I'm determined to make it a good one for Patrick. The holidays have been hard for me for the past few years; our Grandpa Bohn passed away on Christmas Eve in 1999, and so all the stockings and tree trimmings bring a bittersweet feeling for us. My grandpa was always the glue that held our family together, especially during holiday get-togethers, and so it is in his spirit that I am trying my best this Christmas.

But I can't help but let my thoughts linger on how much we'll miss Peter. Believe it or not, he'd always found a way to make it home for Christmas, although I knew that this year, he'd want the holiday leave slots to go to soldiers with sons and daughters of their own. That he was as much of a father figure as Patrick had ever had didn't matter; he wanted to do his part to make sure that all the moms and dads got to see their children over Christmas. It was, in a way, a gift he was giving them.

Still, it's an exciting time for Patrick, who is now eight years old. Being an only child without any older siblings to disabuse him of the notion of Santa Claus, I hope that I can keep the tradition alive another year. All month long I have been sneaking out to buy his presents and squirreling them away in secret hiding places throughout the house. In the days leading up to Christmas Eve, I work hard to wrap the presents as perfectly as I can, as if I were channeling the Christmas spirit in each package. Peter loves Christmas, too, and every Christmas morning he would wake up early with Patrick, sitting down in the glow of the tree and greedily eyeing presents, ready to help Patrick tear them open, even though Peter already knew what was inside.

I plan to have a second family Christmas in July, when Peter gets back from his tour, and everyone approves of this plan. In the meantime, while I'm working on orchestrating a perfect Christmas for Patrick, I'm getting a special holiday care package ready for Peter. I spend time poring over family recipes for Christmas cookies that I think will travel well on the long trip to Baghdad. Anything with chocolate or melty jams are out, but that leaves some of Peter's favorites—Bohn family traditions like sugar cookies with different colored sprinkles, and wreath cookies, which are made up of cornflakes and marshmallows mixed together and twisted into wreaths. Patrick helps me mix in the green food dye and carefully places red hots—for the hollies—onto each wreath.

With the cookies on their cooling racks, I turn my attention to making Peter a scrapbook with photos starting from our childhood and going up to the present. In the front of the scrapbook, I write a long note about our time up north on his leave, and how much the dreams we shared and the promises we made mean to me:

My Dear Brother,

My protector, I wanted to say Thank You. For all the times you have been there for Patrick and I. I will always remember the night we walked to the clearing at the camp. When I look back on it now, I realize that our walk was a metaphor for our lives and the way we chose to live it. We had every reason to be afraid, of real and imagined dangers, but arm-in-arm we walked on. We laughed until we cried, aware of everything. Do you remember when we were young, all the ghosts we battled from under the bed? It seems that we were always fighting for something and trying to protect the ones we love. Stepping down from a challenge and being afraid was never an option. Our battles today are more complicated and filled with difficult decisions. Although I know that I cannot fight all our battles side by side, I want you to know that I will always be there for you no matter what. I promise. As we sat under a million stars that night, I was never afraid. I felt big and small all at the same time, all of the battles significant to reach this point. But mostly I felt safe and secure by your side. There is no one in the world that I trust more then you to sit in the middle of a dark forest and say, "Go ahead, I dare you to." And it is an honor to battle this world at your side; yesterday, today and always.

I wrap up the scrapbook really nicely and put it all into a care package on which I've affixed a little tag that reads in bold writing: DO NOT OPEN UNTIL CHRISTMAS, and I mean it. I want Peter to have something special to open up on Christmas morning, even if he's so far away. As much as I know it's not the same without him here, I know that it must be ten times as bad for him on base. What's it like there, I wonder, for soldiers on Christmas? Do they get extra time to relax? Do they get to uncork a couple bottles of champagne, saved and cooled in the mess for special occasions? I have no idea, but I hope my package will give him something to smile about. I get it to the post office in time for the deadline, knowing it will take three or four weeks to reach him in Iraq.

One of the soldiers has flown on the plane with the casket from Dover Airforce Base in Delaware, so Peter has never been alone. This is a small but necessary comfort for us to hold onto, a sign of respect and thanks from the military, Peter's other family. Our casualty assistance officer explains to us that the honor guard will be with Peter throughout the visitation until the memorial service, never leaving his side unless we request it. It reminds me that we are not the only ones mourning the loss of Peter. That Christmas morning, others lost a brother, too.

Together, we watch the doors close at the back of the hearse, sealing Peter inside.

★ ★ ★

Back at the funeral home, the attendants take the casket inside, and we follow. Thankfully, the media has respected our wishes to stay away during this time, and we have no news vans, no nosey reporters, no onlookers or protestors to contend with. My father and Ted go in to a room with the undertakers first to officially identify Peter's body. Then, the funeral home staff takes some time to clean Peter up before anyone else sees him.

I am the first to go in the room and sit with Peter's body, and I tell my family that I want to go in alone. My footfalls echo around the room, which is all cold steel and hard surfaces. I slowly approach the casket, closing my eyes, squeezing them tight and hoping that when I open them, this will all turn out to be a mistake. I pray to see someone else in there, someone who is not Peter. Instead, when I open my eyes, I am granted and denied my wish all at once. The body lying there is Peter's body, but it is not Peter. It looks, somehow, simultaneously just like him and nothing like him. I know then for the first time that this is truly real, and it starts to sink in. I fall against the casket, putting my head on his still chest, and cry into his uniform. He looks so handsome, so young, so full of promise—all the things that he is. I have to correct myself now: the things that he was. Peter, the Peter I knew and loved, is not here in this room with me. Will never be in this room or any other room with me again.

After fifteen minutes or so alone with Peter, I try asking his spirit for the strength that I will need to get through this next part: explaining everything to Patrick and letting him see Peter's body. As a parent, you're never prepared for your child to suffer. It hurts each time as much as the first time, whether it's a skinned knee, a broken heart, or worse. In the days that followed the announcement of Peter's death, Patrick has fallen into the grip of a terrible insomnia. He thinks that if he falls asleep, he might die like his Uncle Peter. No matter how many times I try to explain it to him, I can't seem to get through to him that he will be fine if he goes to sleep. That he will wake up in the morning. And really, I don't blame him. Who can make any of these promises anymore? Who can go on living as if each day would be the same as the last, as if you'd even get the chance to have another day? After Peter died, I feel as though I can take none of this for granted anymore. But I have to try to make it through for Patrick. If anything is keeping my legs from collapsing, my heart from exploding, it's him, the thought of him, and all the responsibility that I have now to make sure he grows up to keep the spirit of his Uncle Peter alive.

I wipe my eyes, straighten my hair, and go out to meet my son. I take his tiny hand in mine and lead him to Peter, my heart shattering as I feel the pain radiating from him and into me. We step up to the casket, and I put my hand on Peter's chest, trying to help Patrick not be afraid as he looks on.

I grasp for an explanation that will soothe my son's ache. "This is Uncle Peter's body," I say, trying not to choke on my own words. "His soul and his spirit are free now."

I look at Patrick and can see that, like me, like all of us, he understands and he doesn't. I try to take the thought further. "So this is just his shell. But he's still here with us—he can go where he wants. His spirit can choose to stay here with us."

Patrick cries—unstoppable, unflagging tears that

stream down his small red cheeks. I repeat the words to him again, hoping that if I hear it again, I will believe it more. I think of the small sign from the limo and tell him that I know with all my heart that Peter is with us and that he'll never have to leave us again, even though he's left us forever.

★ ★ ★

Later, back at the house, our friends and family join us to keep us company on New Year's Eve, the second occasion that should have been filled with joy and laughter and is instead wracked with heartache and sobs. We wade through the buckets of flowers and piles of casseroles that people have sent over, our hearts struggling to appreciate the kindness of all our caring acquaintances. It is in their company that I start to unravel from the unyielding pressure of the week's events and the day's new wounds. I pour myself glass after glass of wine, reaching for anything that will dull the knives piercing my heart. I curl up on the bathroom floor, too drunk to move, and fall into the deep sleep of grief, knocked into nothingness until my mother finds me, picks me up, and helps move me upstairs and away from the gathering.

TEN

Letting the Media In

As we prepare for Peter's funeral, the question of what to do about all the media attention continues to loom. It's a unanimous decision that we want our privacy during this difficult time, but public interest in the death of a hero is always high, particularly when there are mysterious circumstances. The Army is conducting an autopsy, they report, but by the time we have Peter's public service, there will still be no answers. Our silence only seems to make the force of the questions stronger. What happened to Peter? Why won't you talk to us? the reporters and cameramen ask.

I can't think about other people's feelings right now; my brain is swimming as it is. Acting as the go-between for my parents is exhausting any shred of energy that I still have left in my bones, and it's a struggle just to get up and get myself dressed in the morning. In the days that follow his death, I have recurring dreams that Peter is home, and that none of what we've lived through has been real. It's more like that theater they talk about, the theater of war, where the soldiers are players, and the plot is reversible. I dream that he tells me that he was on a secret mission that we couldn't know about, and he's sorry for all the pain that he caused us, faking his own death. In the dream, I always accept this as truth, and the fog of grief is lifted. When I wake up, in those few brief moments between deep sleep and consciousness, the lines of reality blur, and I truly feel that his death was all a bad dream. Moments later, the constant currents of pain start again, washing over me as I start my day.

I try to hold it together the best I can, mostly because although my brother is gone, my son is still very much here, and he needs me now more than ever. With his primary male role model gone, I'm worried about how Patrick will be able to cope with the life in front of him. It's easy to conjure up catastrophe, to get ahead of myself, to sink into hopelessness as thick as quicksand.

Dealing with the list of tasks leading up to the memorial service is a welcome distraction for me. For the memorial service, we—my cousins and I— pull together a video featuring some of Peter's music and pictures of him. Friends and other family members come over in droves to help put together picture boards for us to put outside at the service, and we crowd around tables and counters putting photos in frames and gathering up already-framed pictures for the service. I make a shadow box full of Peter's medals and commendations, and gather different certificates of achievement to put in a book. It's difficult to look through all of the mementos, but I am on autopilot: I just need to get this done, pure adrenaline powering me through.

At this point, as we're going through all the pictures of Peter's last tour, we start talking about something so obvious I can't believe we've overlooked it: What should we do about the dogs? While Peter is back home with us, two living remnants of his legacy are far away in Baghdad—I worry that Mama and Boris have been left to fend for themselves without Peter to help them. My grief starts to get crowded out by the urgent desire to make Peter's final wishes come true. I need to get those dogs back here safe and sound before anything can take them away, before they can slip off in the night like Peter did, never to be seen or heard from again.

I take a break from cutting and gluing picture boards to contact anyone I can get a hold of back on Peter's old base. Soon, I've heard from a few of his friends who reassure me that they've been taking care of the dogs and that they would try to keep them safe from harm. The soldiers—Dan Haynes, Erik Torres, and Mark Hookano, who have already put their lives on the line to serve their country—write me as much as they can to keep me updated on the dogs: on their whereabouts, on what they've been eating, on how the puppy's skin condition is doing. I am so grateful to them, and in each letter they send, they make sure to tell me how much they're missing Peter, too. Peter was the heart of the group's morale, they say, a constant source of humor and music and love. They tell me that they are haunted by his memory; swear they can hear him coming in between bursts of static on the radio from time to time. For them, the dogs are a connection to the brother they've lost, too. It's a bittersweet connection, but an instant one: I now start to feel I have the military family I have long heard about but never seen.

I am so glad that they are there to keep the dogs safe and loved. They send pictures of themselves playing fetch with Boris, trying to finish teaching him the trick that Peter had been working on. The stubborn puppy can't quite get it, always grabbing the tennis ball and running away.

But I can't get too complacent. Even though it seems far away, I know that soon the unit will come back home, leaving the dogs behind. The military cannot and will not support soldiers bringing back animals from war zones, and I am left with the same concerns I had when Peter was still alive, only without him to talk them over with now. How would I get those dogs—his children, essentially—home?

Now that Peter was gone, who would help me sneak them over the border into Kuwait? Who would make sure they had safe passage back home? I don't know where to even begin to look for the answers to these questions.

As I wring my hands and wonder how on earth I am going to get this last connection to Peter back home to me, I talk my concerns over with my Aunt Julie and my cousins Sarah and Terrie. It is then that we start to hatch a plan at our kitchen table. We can parlay all of the pent-up interest from the media to our advantage, using it to gain the public's attention for the plight of these dogs. Although we have no idea what the fruits of our labor will be, we know that it is better than the alternative, which is staying silent and trying to figure out something on our own. This scheme is out of our comfort zone, over our heads, and well beyond any purview that the military would grant us as survivors of a fallen soldier.

I return a few calls from the local media, explaining that we are willing to speak with them under one condition: The story has to focus on getting Peter's dogs home. They all listen with rapt attention as I tell them about Peter's last months with the dogs and describe all the lengths he had gone to in order to make them as comfortable and safe as possible. I e-mail a few pictures of the dogs, including my favorite ones of Peter holding the puppy, to the news stations, and it isn't long before the camera crews are knocking on the door once again. This time, however, they've been invited in—and they are all clamoring for the heart-warming story about the grieving family who is desperate to bring the beloved dogs of their fallen soldier home from the hot, dry sands of the Middle East.

Soon, our living room is humming with cameras and cables as correspondents crowd in to get their turn with me on camera. It's not natural for me to seek the spotlight, but I keep telling myself that this is all about the dogs, and that thought keeps me centered and sane. I end up being the point person for the interviews, and answer inquiries that come in. The interviews are emotionally excruciating, but I know there's no other way to get the word out about the dogs, so I grin, grit my teeth, and bear it.

Soon, the local segments are picked up by national syndicates. Mama and Boris's story runs on CNN's news loop for a twenty-four-hour period. I get phone calls from relatives and friends, excited that they've seen me on national television. Not believing it even though I know I've done the interviews, I turn on the TV and sit in shock, watching myself talk about my family, my brother, and bringing Mama and Boris home to stay.

ELEVEN

Wish You Were Here

All the attention that the dogs are bringing heightens an already overwhelming tsunami of condolences that are pouring in from all over the world. Thousands of strangers write to us, posting on Peter's death announcement online as well as with the funeral home, expressing their sadness over our loss and telling us we are in their thoughts and prayers.

The words of comfort and support will never bring Peter back, I know, but the kindness of strangers sometimes shines a light in my soul where there has been only darkness since Christmas morning dawned a few weeks before. We have a full day and evening visitation at the funeral home, and thousands of people from our community come, most of whom I've never seen before. I don't think I stop to think, to eat, to use the restroom all day—person after person comes up to me to pay their respects. It's heartbreaking and beautiful all at once; a strange feeling, but a good feeling. I know that no matter how alone I feel, that's not necessarily the case.

But there are costs to opening up our lives to the world, too. The Westboro Baptist Church, a collective of people known for antagonizing all kinds of groups and causes in the name of their own, has found out where and when we'll be holding the public memorial service for Peter. They've made it clear that they plan to be a presence there. Thankfully, the local police department is quick to respond, organizing a huge security effort. They keep tabs on the situation behind the scenes so that we don't have to worry about it, for which I thank them profusely. I don't want this day—this horrible, haunted, beautiful day—to be marred by something as foreign to me as a political protest. For me, Peter's service isn't about either side of an argument—it is about honor and integrity and helping other people, which is how he lived his life. I want his memorial to be a reflection of that, and thanks to the police department's efforts, it looks like that will still be possible.

We've chosen the Grosse Pointe War Memorial as the site of Peter's public service. Since we don't belong to any particular church, it seems the most fitting place, somewhere Peter would have wanted. As we tour the building in preparation for the service, I feel a calm come over me; the memorial is beautiful and looks out through huge picture windows over

WELCOME HOME, MAMA AND BORIS | 107

the waters of Lake St. Clair. It is the perfect place for the public to say their good-byes to Peter—spiritual, simple, and respectful. It also holds a special place in my heart: The room where his funeral will be held is the room where we went to middle-school dances, had our first loves, our first kisses, our first heartbreaks. The symmetry is sad, but appropriate.

When the day comes, I am no more prepared for it than I would be if I had known it was coming for a thousand years. No amount of personal strength or platitudes or positive thinking is going to get me through this day. I stand in front of the mirror that morning, straightening my suit jacket and looking at myself, feeling hollow and not at all a part of what's going on. Our family doctor has prescribed some Valium for me. I take the small white pill in my hand and swallow it down, knowing that it's the only way I will be able to stand up through what the day has in store for me.

★ ★ ★

Our family is instructed by the funeral home to get to the memorial first, well before the crowds. The West-boro Baptist Church people are already there holding their signs, but because of the security efforts of the Patriot Guard Riders—a group of motorcycle riders who oppose Westboro's protests—who have shown up, as well as the police—they have everything timed down to the minute and have blocked off a secure entrance for us—I don't even notice them there. I don't hear them; I don't see them. I read about it in the papers in the days to come, but for now, they are not here. I am already feeling the effects of the Valium, my knees steely and wobbly all at once. I try to keep my breathing steady; it feels tinny in my ears, roaring like the ocean. It is all I can hear, and I feel nothing and everything.

Before the throngs of people arrive, our family is given two separate rooms to sit and rest in before the service. My mother and her family are in one, my father and his family in the other. Just as has been my role so far, I move on autopilot as the caretaker, the go-between. I move from room to room making sure that everyone is okay—a futile effort, but one I have to make. Patrick moves between the two rooms, too, sticking close by my side and squeezing my hand the whole time.

As the clock ticks closer to the start of the service, the cavernous service hall fills up. Within minutes, it's filled to capacity. People spill out into the entrance and into the garden and in back of the building. There are veterans, families of departed soldiers, families of soldiers still overseas, friends, family, neighbors, strangers, each one with a hand to press into ours and a message of thankfulness for Peter and his life. I think about how sad it is that Peter, who always wanted to make a difference but never thought he was good enough, was the only person who wouldn't be around to see the crowds of people aching to tell him how good he really was. I hope that he can see us from where he is, and thinking back to the limo ride the other day, I think that maybe, just maybe, he can.

When I can put it off no longer, I lead my family's long walk to the front of the room, where we have seats roped off for us. I try to take deep breaths and look down at my feet, watching myself put one foot in front of the other in an effort to keep walking straight into an uncertain future. We take our seats, and I listen to Air Force Chaplain Lt. Col. Harold B. Owens, a man I work with in hospice and asked to perform the service, begin the readings.

The texts that he shares are so relevant to Peter and his memory, and I am insanely grateful that he has agreed to perform the service rather than a stranger. As the Wing Chaplain of the 180th Fighter Wing out of Toledo, Ohio, he also knows firsthand the sacrifice that men like Peter give for their country. First, his clear voice rings out in the crowded hall as he reads the Prayer of St. Francis of Assisi, the patron saint of animals:

> *Lord, make me an instrument of your peace.*
> *Where there is hatred, let me sow love;*

where there is injury, pardon;
where there is doubt, faith;
where there is despair, hope;
where there is darkness, light;
and where there is sadness, joy.
O Divine Master, grant that I may not so much seek
to be consoled as to console;
to be understood as to understand;
to be loved as to love.
For it is in giving that we receive;
it is in pardoning that we are pardoned;
and it is in dying that we are born to eternal life.

Next, equally as appropriate is the U.S. Soldier's Creed, the promise of service that Peter made in his life and now would continue to fulfill in death. I struggle not to feel bitter as I think of that promise as the one that eventually would take my brother away from me. Instead, I try to think of it as a reminder of all the honorable things he chose to do, and what a wonderful person he was. It makes me feel like he's watching over us still, hearing the chaplain speak the words:

I am an American Soldier.
I am a Warrior and a member of a team.
I serve the people of the United States, and
live the Army Values.
I will always place the mission first.

I will never accept defeat.
I will never quit.
I will never leave a fallen comrade.
I am disciplined, physically and mentally tough,
trained and proficient in my warrior tasks and drills.
I always maintain my arms, my equipment and myself.
I am an expert and I am a professional.
I stand ready to deploy, engage, and destroy, the enemies of
the United States of America in close combat.
I am a guardian of freedom and the American way of life.
I am an American Soldier.

My heart thunders in my chest as it becomes my turn to take the podium. But suddenly, as quickly as the thumping began, it seems to subside. I go entirely numb as I stand to speak to a crowd of hundreds about a loss so fresh I'm still struggling to come to grips with it. Because words will never begin to express the grief I feel over Peter's death, it's as if my mind and body shut off the part of me that would be affected by these words, my words, which I can't believe I'm about to say.

"On behalf of Peter's family, I would like to thank you all for being here today. It means so much to all of us," I begin, staring out at the crowd, watching their faces melt into one another, combine into nothing more than a sea of colors in an unfamiliar room. Behind me, the winter winds ripple Lake St. Clair, and the stormy skies cast a gray pallor on everyone through the large windows.

But this feeling is not what's on the paper in front of me, this is not what I can say to these people who have come to pay their respects, the only currency the living have in a time like this. So I go on with what I've written in my shaky handwriting. "As I look out at all of your faces, all the memories are coming rushing back again and I want to thank you for all those moments," I say, looking into the rows of family members in whom I can see glimmers of Peter—in my father's nose, in Patrick's eyes.

Peter was my little brother who thought he was my big brother. And it didn't seem to matter where I went, inevitably I would run into someone who knew one of my brothers, and affectionately I was known often only as Peter or Ted's sister. I was always the quiet one, the wallflower, and it was my brothers that shone, and I am feeling very out of place up here.

For a moment, the truth rings out in that room, and I feel a small trickle of strength to go on.

For those of you who don't already know, Peter and I shared a birthday. We often joked about how we were meant to have been twins. Growing up we

*Peter's second album cover—
with a photo of him hamming
it up, age five.*

Peter, Carey, and baby Patrick.

*Peter smiling proudly
in his Army t-shirt.*

Carey and Peter,
Christmas, 2006.

Peter entertaining troops in Iraq.

Peter hanging out with some interpreters in Baghdad.

Peter on patrol in Kuwait.

Peter on patrol in Baghdad.

Peter feeding Mama and Boris.

Peter with the doghouse he built for Mama and her pups.

Peter and Boris, new best friends.

Boris on the streets of Baghdad.

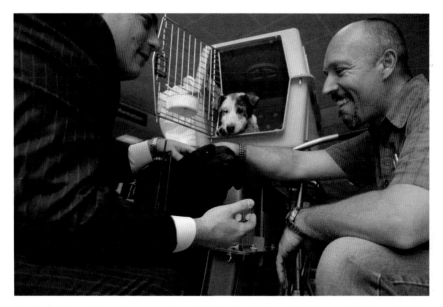

Justin Harlem (l), assistant to Sen. Carl Levin (MI), with Mama, Boris and Rich Crook, at Dulles Airport, Washington, D.C. © Molly Wald

Boris after his first bath in Pennsylvania. © Molly Wald

Mama explores the hotel room in Pennsylvania. © Molly Wald

Mama and Boris—almost home.
© Molly Wald

Welcome home, Mama & Boris!
Mama gives Rich a big thank you.
© Molly Wald

Carey, Rich, and Mama share
an embrace. © Molly Wald

Carey and Patrick meet Boris. © *Molly Wald*

Home at last. Mama and Boris relax with family members (left to right), Christine Neesley, Patrick, Julie Dean (aunt), Sarah Kelson (cousin), and Carey. © *Molly Wald*

Aymen Murrani visits Carey and the dogs, 2009.

Peter's tree on Warrior's Walk, Fort Stewart, GA.

A portrait of Peter painted by an Iraqi interpreter.

Dog tags—Sgt. Peter C. Neesley. © Amanda Friedman

Carey, Patrick, Mama, Boris, & Razia, Spring 2013. © Amanda Friedman

were the very best of friends. We battled monsters under the bed together, fought off the forces of evil in the pine trees in the backyard, and got into a lot of trouble together.

Peter was my best friend; he was my touchstone. Peter was there for every important moment, every transition, every heartache. He always knew exactly what I needed without me having to say a word. Peter was there when my son was born. And he made one of the two most incredible uncles ever. He was the closest thing to a father my son has ever had. He was the proudest uncle on the planet, and he spoiled Patrick to no end. Patrick was the light in his eyes, and he is Patrick's hero. I cannot thank him enough for the difference he made and will continue to make in Patrick's life.

As I speak of Peter's commitment to friends and family, I see evidence of it gathered in the room, both in people who loved Peter and whom Peter loved, as well as people Peter would never meet. I tell them about Peter's talents, which many of them already know much about: his music, his sailing, his outdoorsmanship. I speak of how loyal and protective he was, how compassionate and courageous he was. How he defined unconditional love. How he stood up for what he believed in until the very end. I think of the people of Iraq, the last people to see him alive and benefit from this commitment to do the right thing. I think of Mama and Boris, worlds away from us and needing our love now as much as we need theirs, as I say:

> *Some may say Peter was a bit dramatic, but Peter lived his life with such a tremendous passion that everything became larger than life for him. He felt everything so deeply. He befriended so many and would move mountains to try to make things just a little easier for them. He couldn't stand to see anyone in pain or suffering. He was known to show up at any given time with someone who was having a hard time and open his heart and home to them until they could stand on their feet again. This was true of people and animals. And he would fight for them forever.*

I make a promise to Peter to continue this fight, my resolve to bring Mama and Boris home strengthening even as, on the surface, I become weaker, float farther away from myself.

> *The world seems a little less bright now. I am still hoping to wake up from this horrible nightmare. I have to believe that someone or something must have needed him pretty badly to take him away so abruptly from us. There are moments when I am overcome with grief, there are moments when I am*

angry, and there are times when I'm just numb and I wander the world in complete disbelief that he isn't coming home. But he has a new home now, and I am confident that he is in the arms of his grandparents and all the soldiers and friends that left before he did.

I take one last pause, not daring to look up at the crowd, lest I lose the false footing I've gained thanks to the Valium and the surreal tenor of the day. I leave them all with some parting words of advice that I think Peter would have agreed with, my fingers rubbing over the words on the page as I try to come to grips with them for myself. I will need these in the future, I say to myself. I will need to follow my own advice.

I think what he would want you all to take away from this tragic end is to appreciate every day you are given. Tomorrow is promised to no one. He would want you all to go on and become the best person you can be, to chase your dreams. He would want you to appreciate every sunrise and sunset. Every star lit at night. He would want you to tell the people who are important to you that you love them. He would want you to reach out to those in pain and offer them a hand. We were so blessed to have had him in our lives, as brief as it may have been. I am so grateful for the time I had with my little big brother. I will think of him every day for the rest of my life, and I will try to honor his memory by being everything he would have wanted me to be.

After a few more moments, a few more words, I sit down, not even feeling the chair underneath me. My family and friends are all here by my side, but I can't see them; it's like I have blinders on, like I've fashioned my own little bubble. The rest of the service is beautiful: my father speaks, a general reads from the service that Peter's unit had for him in Iraq. The general quotes from Peter's friend and fellow soldier, Dan Haynes, who calls Peter one of the best friends he has ever had, a talented musician, and a stand-up man. Later, Peter's best friend Evan along with some of his other friends stand up to perform Pink Floyd's "Wish You Were Here," a perfect tribute to Peter's memory and music, one of the things he loved the most. The melancholy chorus runs through me like water, like the unending rivers of my sadness—how I wish you were here.

★ ★ ★

The service ends, complete with full honors from the military—the folding and presentation of the flags, the playing of "Taps," and a 21-gun salute all pay homage to Peter's last actions and intentions to protect his country. The gunfire catches me off guard; I feel like I've been shot through the chest as the salute echoes through the cold marble of the assembly hall.

Although the service is done, a long day of mourning still stretches out before us. We have to stop at the funeral home before one last small service for our family at the Bayview Yacht Club, where we all sailed together as children. This stop at the funeral home is the last time that we will be able to see Peter, because as soon as we can reclaim his organs from the Army after their investigation, he will be cremated. It is unbearable to think about the fact that my brother is not whole in his casket, and I want everything to be as perfect as I can possibly make it, not for appearances but to honor his memory properly. As I peer down at him in the casket, I start to cry as I fix his hair. A concerned funeral attendant comes over and asks me not to do that, but I insist: his hair is wrong. His part should be like this. It should be like this in the front. This is not how he wears it. I cannot bring myself to use the past tense.

I nearly crawl into the casket with him, try to disappear with him. I sob and kiss him and hold him and tell him again and again how much I love him. These feel like the last words I will be able to speak for quite some time. I can feel my body shutting down, my brain clicking off, my heart closing itself off.

After the final service, we go back to the funeral

home to get all of the flowers that have been donated. Although we have requested donations for the rescue of the dogs instead, people have still sent a sea of flowers—brightly colored, sickly sweet-smelling arrangements that we now have to wrangle into our family's van. My cousin Michael helps me carry some of the bigger arrangements out to the car, and while we are lugging the bouquets, he tries to reach out and make me feel better in any way he can. He can see I'm a shell of myself, can see the toll today has taken on me.

We make it to the van, almost toppling over from the weight of the flowers. It's amazing, really, how heavy they are, all the little petals combining to feel like dumbbells in our arms. As Michael stuffs an arrangement into the back of the van, he says to me, "Carey, what you said in there today was so beautiful. Peter would be so proud of you."

And as he says this, a single red rose falls out over his shoulder and right into my hands. Our jaws drop at the timing of the moment. "That's from Peter," he says, and as the tears fall down my cheeks and onto the flower, I know this is true.

TWELVE

If I Can Only Find a Way

After the funeral, I stumble around like a newborn foal, confounded and a little in awe of everything. How am I going to live my life now? Do I really have to keep getting up in the morning, going about my business, getting older, moving on? I spend a lot of time thinking about Peter, about the things that he will miss. How he'll never get to play his guitar again, or how I'll never get to hear him play it. How he won't be on the sidelines at Patrick's lacrosse games. The world without Peter seems gray, dark, and unfamiliar.

Still, I have responsibilities to people. I am determined to be a good mother, to give my son a stable home. I drive to work each day to help hospice patients, some of whom have lived through more grief than I could ever imagine. They need me, and sometimes I can feel Peter working through them, communicating with me, reminding me to enjoy my every moment on this Earth and all the small gifts that come with those moments. I white-knuckle my way through each day, hoping that the next one might go down a little easier.

I see very quickly that the universe is not done with me, though. The media interviews have continued, bringing with them a seemingly never-ending barrage of e-mails, calls, and letters from around the world. John Rutherford at NBC writes a big feature on his website, *The Huffington Post* chimes in, and pretty soon if you type "Peter Neesley" into any search engine, the story of Mama and Boris is the first thing to come up. The clips that made it to the national news didn't feature any of that information, so I'm even more surprised by the sheer number of messages that have found their way to us. People had not only come to care about the story, but they had also done some digging to get our contact information— an indication of how deeply the story has touched those who sent a missive our way.

My cousin Sarah set up a small website with pictures of Peter and the dogs and a summary of the story, as well as a Yahoo e-mail address to which people could write to inquire about the dogs and how they could help. With my Aunt Julie and cousins Sarah and Terrie helping me at first, I go through the e-mail for hours a day as a part of my routine for this new, strange world I find myself living in.

Once the trickle of e-mails starts, it quickly pro-
gresses to a flood. Many of them are from people who
recommend I look into various news stories as well
as a popular autobiography recently published by a
Marine who rescued a dog from Iraq. Most of them
offer money, even though it's obvious that the writers
don't have much to give—something that touches me
deeply. All of them are supportive and gracious.

"God bless you, I will be praying you succeed,"
one woman writes, offering her thoughts and prayers
as the currency to help us in our mission.

"I don't have much, but I'd like to give what I
can," another says, and I can tell he means it.

E-mail after e-mail comes in offering sympathy,
prayers, and suggestions. Like me, most of the writers
haven't a clue where to start. They have no idea what
the mission will entail, they say, and I can sympathize,
even though I'm in the middle of it. I feel like I'm in
over my head, more worried about what will happen
to the dogs as each day goes by, but not any more sure
of what to do next. I try to turn my worry over to
Peter, try to ask him what I should do. I grasp for any
possible connection that I can find to anyone who
may be able to help me.

As the e-mails continue to rain down from everywhere, I am sending out pleas of my own. I write often
to check in with the soldiers on Peter's base who have
been taking care of Mama and Boris, trying to feed

them when they can and keep an eye on them. Clearly, this is no easy task; Mama and Boris are feral, and even when Peter was there to look after them, they would fend for themselves on the city streets all day long before returning to their house. Sometimes, the soldiers say, days go by between sightings of the dogs. Or they'll see the puppy, but miss seeing the mother. Several times a day, I reach out into the universe, searching for someone to listen to my prayer to keep these dogs safe. They are all I have left of my brother, and I desperately need them to come home to me.

It's so hard for me to deal with the silences and spotty communication, sometimes stretching for days, coming to me from the base. In the war zone, the men have their hands full with so much—but for me, this has become my whole life. Sometimes, if they aren't able to access the Internet, I will go days without having answers to my questions, or thoughts on my theories about how we're going to get the dogs home. If my world were normal, if things were sane, I wouldn't be living and dying by the computer, hanging on every word sent from men thousands of miles away with bigger things on their mind. But this is my new normal—this is my reality now.

Some days, it feels like my sole purpose, and when I'm awake in the middle of the night or catching up on sleep during my lunch break, my internal clock resets to Baghdad time. Between planning everything that remains for Peter—arranging for his cremation and interment, dealing with the Army for such matters as pension and autopsy reports, and eventually sorting through his belongings—including my unopened Christmas package—and dealing with the dogs, I am caught between worlds, stretched thin. I'm so thankful to have the help of my aunt and cousins, who can take over the e-mail account if I need them to, or help me field some of the phone calls or ask some of the questions that I need to ask in the days and weeks to come.

Their support is crucial to me as we sort through the possibilities—and the impossibilities—as well as the inevitable disappointments that come up. Some hot leads fizzle out to dead ends. One woman located in Baghdad seems to be on board to help, only to leave us in the lurch when she realizes that Peter has already passed away and is not on base. A surprising thing happens to me then. Although life has thrown way too much at me, already, I somehow find the strength to press on. I am surprised at how driven I am, at how confident I am that I can get this done. Failure isn't an option—I need to find a way. If one person can't help me, I commit myself to finding another one who can.

One day, word comes from Dan, Erik, and Mark that Mama had been missing for several days. My heart contracts into a tight fist and does not release until I read on that they've found her. They write that she's currently under Peter's trailer—inside the walls of the base, where he used to lay his head each night. That Mama found her way inside the base and could sneak in the locked fortress is the first thing I can't quite wrap my mind around. The other is the recognition of an uncanny coincidence, something that, the more I think about it, seems less and less like a coincidence at all, and more like something she must have known, a homing instinct set deep inside her heart. She had never been to Peter's trailer, and had no way of knowing that it was his; nothing was there to distinguish it from all the others save for whatever lingering remnants of Peter's scent remained. She must have followed it there, I think.

The soldiers report that they can't get her to come out; it is as though she is in mourning, sitting watchfully over her master's domain now that he has passed. She wouldn't accept food or water for seven or eight days, until one day, when she was finally ready, she shook the dust off her legs and returned to her puppy. It reminds me of how I feel when I see Patrick—the light left in his eyes is what keeps me going every day, keeps me from shrinking down into my shell and hiding in my bed. I think that maybe, one day as Mama has done, I'll be able to say good-bye to some of my sadness, or at the very least, find a way to live with it.

The story strengthens my resolve to bring these animals home—if I can only find a way.

THIRTEEN

Angels from Nowhere

With Sarah's help, we set up a donation site. After reading from so many people that they'd be willing to donate funds to the cause—and knowing that the task is probably going to be as expensive as it is monumental—I am eager to accept all the help that these kind strangers are offering. The donations, like the e-mails, come from all over the world—from the heartland and places like where Peter and I grew up to more exotic locales. As weak as I feel sometimes, it gives me strength to know that this story has registered as an important one for so many people. I am hoping with every ounce of my soul that I get to write a happy ending.

Although most of the e-mails come with the caveat in bold letters that the senders have no connections outside of their own community, there are diamondlike glimmers of knowledge to be gleaned. Some people write to advise us to contact our local representatives, even giving us links to websites where we can get petitions going. Others write with helpful links carrying information about the legal hurdles and red tape that we'll need to be prepared to cut through—forms that will need to be filled out and filed with the Centers for Disease Control. One day, I log on to check for the day's tips and to respond with thanks to all those who have sent messages, and find a tip from a kind woman offering not a personal connection, but a place to start: "I don't know if this will help, but if anyone can get this process moving, I would tell you to contact Best Friends Society in Utah. They have an amazing network in place all over the world."

I am intrigued. I've never heard of the Best Friends Society, but after some quick research, I find that the tip is right on the money. Their website is full of testimonials from all of the people they've helped with their worldwide rescue network—and what speaks volumes to me, as an animal lover, are the words of thanks that go unspoken by the countless animals they've given new lives to.

While I'm at home holding my breath between phone calls from possible sources of help and juggling my responsibilities as a mother with my job, the fates appear to be conspiring in our favor. Soon, I'm in contact with a man named Rich Crook, who is the Rapid Response Manager for Best Friends. Immediately, I'm intrigued by his title; it feels almost military in scope, perfect for our mission, I think. Rich has heard our story on CNN and writes to tell me that he would be more than happy to help us in any way he can. While it's heartening to read this from the legions of supportive strangers who have reached out to us following Peter's death, to hear something like this from Rich, who can actually offer tangible help, feels like nothing short of a godsend.

I get to know Rich a little more throughout our correspondence, and hearing his story, I know that to call our meeting a lucky break was a colossal understatement. Rich is a kind, gentle man with a passion for helping both people and animals. He hails from Michigan originally, in a town not far from my own. I feel an instant connection with him in our letters and phone calls, and his positive energy is infectious, buoying my spirits during the rough ride we know we have ahead.

Before he became involved with Best Friends, Rich had a long career as a firefighter. It doesn't surprise me to hear that he has dedicated his life to helping people in distress. In 2005, when Hurricane Katrina devastated the Gulf Coast, Rich felt a calling to go down and help. He made his way down to the flooded, otherworldly wreckage of a once-vibrant area, and while he was down there, was moved by the plight of not just the human residents of the Gulf, but also by the thousands of animals who were orphaned, lost, or unable to be cared for by their embattled owners. His position with Best Friends quickly changed from volunteer to staff member, as he pioneered the rapid response division, something sort of like FEMA for animals. He made a name for himself pulling puppies and cats from the murky floodwaters, and knew very quickly that this was how he needed to spend the rest of his life. Even as the muddy streets started to reappear and the Gulf started to rebuild, Rich knew that there would be other emergencies, other creatures in need. He sends me some pictures of himself in the field—man's best friend's best friend.

After Katrina, Rich relocated to Utah to work with Best Friends full time. The stories that he tells me of his rescues make my logistical difficulties look small, if only for a second. His attitude gives me hope—if there's a will, there's a way, he says, and I know I've got will on my side. He tells me about a rescue he ran a few years before, when he and his team were in Lebanon helping to start a spay-and-neuter program and a shelter. As tensions in the region ran high and firefights between enemy groups heightened, his team began to airlift dogs to the United States, a rescue operation that eventually saved five thousand dogs.

"So what do we need to do?" I ask, my mind going a thousand miles an hour, my body essentially running in place.

"Honestly, I don't know," he began, really mulling it over. "But what I do know is that there's something we can do."

The next time we speak, he has mapped out a logistical plan—or, in our case, a set of problems we'd need to solve. We would need security clearance to get on the base, get the dogs, and bring them to the border. We would need a team to handle the transportation. We would need a vet in Iraq to clear the dogs for crossing the border. Then, we'd need an airline that could fly into and out of Iraqi airspace. The dogs couldn't make any direct flights from Iraq to the States, so we'd need an airline to transport them from Kuwait, where the first airline would drop them off, to Washington, D.C., where they'd have to stay in quarantine before making the final leg of their journey to Michigan.

And that's just the bare-bones list, Rich warns us. It's hard not to get discouraged when we see the concrete steps mapped in front of us, especially since there's no accounting for all of the horrible ways that things could possibly go wrong. My mind turns to a dark place, thinking about how the universe hasn't been too kind to my family and me lately. But signs from Peter continue to pop up—I see him everywhere, in the stars, in the snow, in a pair of swans I see walking by the war memorial, and most of all, in Rich and his energy.

"Are you up for this?" Rich asks. I don't even need to think about my answer.

There is much to be feared about the unknown, about what might happen to derail our best-laid plans. But there's more than darkness in the unknown. Sometimes, there is unbelievable light, too. One ray of light comes in the form of John Wagner, the Vice

President of Gryphon Airlines, who e-mails me out of the blue after seeing one of the stories about Peter and the dogs on the news.

Like most Americans, I'd never heard of Gryphon. It's not an airline that you'll find at your regional airport. As I'm learning more about the military world, I'm also learning about the intricate web of private contractors who support the military's operations. Soldiers like Peter aren't the only ones who are charged with dismantling and rebuilding the war zones in Iraq and Afghanistan. Gryphon Airlines, John explains, flies cargo and contractors into and out of Iraq for the military and other defense companies. They are also, he says, the only civilian airline allowed in or out of Iraq.

I can't believe how quickly this first piece is falling into place. I write to Rich to let him know about the exciting news. John makes it clear that he'll do whatever he can to get those dogs out of there, free of charge. My jaw drops when I read that. To know that such generosity is coming to me from someone I hadn't even known existed only hours before is humbling. Suddenly, we can cross flying into and out of Iraq off our list.

But the list is a long one, and we have many things still to cross off. There is no roadmap for how to pull dogs out of an active war zone, but I rest a little easier that night, knowing that two angels from nowhere have appeared to help light the way.

FOURTEEN

Saints and Saviors

With Rich Crook organizing the rescue and John Wagner from Gryphon volunteering to handle transportation out of Iraq, I am in a position I'd never thought I'd be in: one with some measure of hope. With this hope, though, comes the fear of letting everyone down—especially Peter. With each rung on the ladder we climb, the harder the fall down might hurt. My heart still feeling torn to pieces over Peter's loss, and unable to find closure without the answers I'm seeking from the Army or a proper burial, my grief still hangs in the air like the oppressive heat before a thunderstorm, and I can find no release for it. The closest I can come is by working on this mission.

Our next stumbling block comes as we try to find proper veterinary care for Mama and Boris. While I wish it were as simple as making sure they are healthy enough to complete the journey, such a diagnosis would be a luxury at this point. We are legally obligated to have the proper shots and international health certificates required to fly. Even if we can talk the airlines into overlooking the requirement, which is unlikely, it is the only way that the Centers for Disease Control will allow the dogs to enter the United States. To have them turned away after such an improbable journey is not an option.

Some days, it feels like time is whizzing by, and I'm caught up in a whirlwind of things to do, people to talk to, and e-mails to answer. But some days, it feels like time has slowed to an agonizing crawl. I know that the military will only turn a blind eye for so long—if we can't get those dogs out of there, their fate will be damned. Although they are unable to help us on an institutional level, I do appreciate everything that the military is doing to let things slide and not pay attention. And individually, Peter's friends in the unit are still doing their best to make sure that the dogs are safe, or at least relatively safe. It brings a smile to my otherwise darkened face to know that the soldiers are gaining some comfort from the dogs, too—their last connection to Peter, the friend and brother they loved just as much as I did, even though they'd only known him a short while.

When Mama makes a second disappearing act, I am frantic with worry that something has happened to her at the hands of those who might be following orders. But Peter's friends make it clear to me that the puppy is still alive and accounted for, and they don't know of anyone who would have euthanized or executed Mama. I take the small comfort where I can, but I am always teetering on a thin line between sanity and hysteria, tipped over by the smallest kernel of thought that expands to a boulder-size worry. As I know all too well from my experience with Peter, once something is gone, it doesn't matter how unreal it feels—that's the reality. This war is no play; Iraq is no theater; and the dead will not return.

Thankfully, Dan, Mark, and Erik write soon with the news that they've located Mama. A small reconnaissance mission reveals that an Iraqi general had found Mama, and taken her back to his home. He was caring for her well—feeding her, making sure she got outside time, and most important, keeping her out of the road and the path of trucks and tanks—but ultimately, keeping her away from the base as well.

I try to tell myself that this man is a kind and decent person, although I've never met him and don't know the first thing about him. The confounding thing is that I am not the only one in the dark—so is everyone else, even the men who have found him and seen him with Mama. There is an understandable lack of trust that exists in these relationships with strangers, but there's also a kind of blind faith that happens. I try to cling to that blind faith, choosing to believe that people can be good. Lately, there have been so many affirmations of that.

As it turns out, this general is another one of those good people. The soldiers speak to him about the dog, and at first, he is adamant—Mama is his dog, and he is caring for her. But then, as he takes the time to listen to them and the story unfolds, the whole wonderful, horrible, sad, beautiful tale, he agrees that Mama must make it home with her pup to Peter's family. He doesn't stop there, but offers whatever help he can to our mission. I sit at my computer screen, reading this story of generosity, and my heart bursts with gratitude for someone I will never meet. I don't even know his name. But when I see what he's done for me, I send my thanks up to the heavens and over the seas to wherever he is.

Still, my ears are ringing with the ticking of the clock. About two weeks have passed since we snagged a huge break with Gryphon Airlines, but we still need to conquer this next step. We desperately cast about for a connection to any veterinarians in Iraq who might be able to get anywhere near the base. This is one of the cases where being in a war zone definitely complicates matters—access to veterinary care isn't exactly priority number one. The grassroots nature of our mission never escapes me, particularly during this part of the search. We are relying on the kindness of strangers, the randomness of connections, and the tenuous strings that hold together the world in wartime to get us through. As we create this roadmap, the universe continues to hand us the lights to guide us.

"I'm not sure this will be of any help," writes a woman named Gretchen Biery, a U.S. government employee in Afghanistan. "But I read the article about your desire to bring home your brother's adorable dogs from Iraq. I found your e-mail address with the pictures. I live in Afghanistan, where there is a small animal shelter that, among other things, helps people here organize taking adopted pets abroad from Afghanistan. This made me wonder if there's anything like this in Iraq. I looked on the Web and found an international Society for the Protection of Animals site, which listed one person as their contact in Iraq. I wonder if this person could help you in some way? I wish you the best of luck."

Even though this woman didn't have a direct connection to this person, at least we had a starting point. She had pointed us in the general direction of the proverbial needle, even though she couldn't drag it out of the haystack. That part was up to us.

My cousins and I started researching the Murrani family, who ran the Society for the Protection of Animals, finding any article online that we could that had to do with them or their work. Farah's parents, Khalid and Tawheed, are both doctors of veterinary medicine, and have been prominent animal advocates in Iraq throughout the years. I read that they were instrumental in shaping the Baghdad Zoo, which, before we bombed Iraq in 2003, was home to over six hundred species of animals spread out over two hundred acres. The family had been involved in rebuilding the zoo when it was destroyed during the start of the war. Tears easily come to my eyes as I read that all but thirty-five animals died in the bombing. I think of Peter and how horrified he would have been by that troubling reality of war, just as he was whenever he came across an injured child or civilian who had been caught in the unavoidable cross fire. His spirit seems to be pointing me toward these people as I read more about the kindnesses they've extended to local animals—they actually run the Iraq Society for Animal Welfare, Iraq's humane society. The match couldn't be more perfect.

There is only one problem: We haven't found their contact information yet. But with so much press devoted to them, we know it can be only a matter of time until we dig up some kind of address or phone number. I have no other choice but to believe this, and I stay up late into the night, searching and poring over articles and links.

One day, there it is: the needle. I gleefully pull it out of the haystack of pixels heaped upon my screen and start typing, copying Rich on the exchange so that he can weigh in and help, too.

"Dear Dr. Murrani," I write to Farah, trying to sound as polite, humble, and appreciative as I possibly can, and I curse the limitations of e-mail for not letting me convey my desperation and deservedness. If she could only meet us, I think as I frantically type out my supplication. "I'm the sister of fallen soldier Peter Collins Neesley, who died while serving overseas in Baghdad. He loved your country and always spoke so highly of the wonderful people he would meet there while he was out rebuilding the communities. The reason why I am writing to you is that I am hoping you can help us rebuild our family."

I sit for what feels like hours, writing and rewriting, typing and deleting. I don't want to say the wrong thing. I feel like I am so close to a breakthrough, to let this slip through my fingers would be the end of me. I try to think of Peter standing behind me, cracking jokes and playing his guitar. The words come a little easier. Before I know it, I am clicking "send," casting my pleas and prayers out into the universe to what I hope will be a sympathetic friend.

It's not long before there's a response waiting in my inbox. At first I am afraid to open it, because I know that once I have, whatever is contained inside will be real. Whether I like it or not. Whether it's the saving grace I need or the damnation I so fear. Fragile as I am, I almost burst into tears when I read that Dr. Murrani is no longer in Iraq; she's doing animal welfare work in South Africa now. But the e-mail doesn't end there, and so neither does my hope. "My family is still in Iraq. I am pretty sure that they can help you. I'm going to give you my brother's e-mail. Why don't you write to him, and see what he can do? I wish you luck."

I know that I will need what feels like much more than luck. But at the same time, it feels like luck might be all that I need.

I send an e-mail off to her brother, explaining the situation. I am absolutely floored when I get an e-mail back from someone named Aymen Murrani, saying simply, enthusiastically, blessedly: "Of course we will help you!"

Rich and I e-mail back and forth with Aymen, who, as it happens, is a sixteen-year-old boy and part of the answer to one of our biggest problems. He is brave, generous, and wise beyond his years. As we are corresponding with him, we get to know him a little and easily fall in love with this young soul who represents so much hope for his country. I know that, wherever Peter is, he's watching and smiling that we've made this particular friend at this particular time. Knowing that Aymen is out there gives me hope, not just for our situation, but also for the future. I feel the same way about my own son, who is growing up so fast—I try not to miss those moments with him as I'm engrossed by this mountainous mission to get his uncle's furry friends home to our family.

It turns out that Aymen's parents are both vets, and so he handles communication between us and them, acting as translator and project manager, keeping track of what forms we're going to need, what vaccines we'll need, and so on. I am terrified when I hear that they plan to drive across the city—which is a dangerous proposition on a good day—to get the vaccines that the dogs will need from a local clinic. If something happens to them, I think, I'll never forgive myself. But still, they want to do this, and there's no stopping them. When I hear they've made it back safely, I am relieved and send a prayer of thanks up to Peter, who I feel must be their protector, their soldier in spirit.

One day, I ask Aymen why on earth he would stick his neck out so far to help people he's never met. I'm not fishing for declarations of loyalty, but I am genuinely curious. I think about how I've lived my life, and hope that if the tables were turned, I'd be able to be at least half as generous. The reason is simple, he says. Aymen and his brother Saud are big supporters of the United States' mission in their country, and have spent some time working with the Army as interpreters. "I'm in support of what your brother tried to do here," he said.

I have heard this a million times before by people who have expressed sorrow over Peter's loss, and I know that it is always heartfelt, certainly. But somehow, hearing it from this Iraqi teenager is partic-ularly mind-blowing. He tells me without reservation that working with the U.S. Army has meant the world to him and his brother because they are aware of all the sacrifices the soldiers are making for them—for a country of people they might never meet. "I never met your brother," he points out. "But I'd still like to help him. I'd like to help you."

I ask him about his family, making sure that he isn't going against his parents' wishes to help us. He is putting not only himself, but his parents, in harm's way by actively associating with the U.S. military, not to mention crossing dangerous stretches of land that are riddled with mines, IEDs, and people with dark, desperate motives. He explains that at first his father was a little tentative, just because of the dangers that couldn't necessarily be mitigated, all of those terri-ble unknowns. I can't blame him, my brother hav-ing fallen victim to such an unknown. But eventually, Aymen says, his father gave his blessing. "You need to go do this," he told Aymen and Saud.

Although this mission is the largest in scope they'd done, the family had been involved in other, similar rescues, using underground and backdoor channels to get dogs safely out of harm's way. The Murrani family was also the recipient of a grant from the U.S. mili-tary to try to start spay-and-neuter programs in Iraq, something that is desperately needed as hundreds of feral animals roam the streets untended to. All of this good work has given them some connections and experience within the country, which will be invaluable to our mission.

The vaccines are expensive by virtue of the war—what we pay $50 for in the States, they would pay $200 or more per vaccine—and when Aymen and his mom go to fetch the vaccines, their connections help them get the rare medicine where others cannot. I am humbled when I hear the cost of the medications and know that the Murranis paid for them up front without any promise of repayment, and I make sure they know how resolved I am to pay them back.

At night, I always watch the news, and I check blogs and news sites between answering e-mails from the thousands of generous strangers who continue to donate small amounts to Peter's dogs. Money orders come in from as far as the Grand Cayman Islands and New Zealand, exotic places that I've never been and can't even imagine as I live through another Michigan winter. It's hard not to miss the vitriol that is spewed from both sides of every debate, especially as politicians scramble to ingratiate themselves to voters. The war, for many people, is a political situation—something they can never touch, or feel, but have impassioned opinions about.

I can't stick with one story for too long; it makes me too sad. Because I know things that I wouldn't wish on my own worst enemy. I know how it feels to lose your brother, your best friend. I know how it feels to cry yourself to sleep, to wake in the night feeling like you can't breathe, the weight of unanswered questions sitting heavily on your chest.

But when I look at the e-mails and notes from Aymen and his family, in particular, I am reminded that I also know things about this war and this world that others haven't had the good fortune to experience, either. I know that in the middle of the fighting, in the midst of all the talk of "good" and "evil," of "wrong" and "right," there are people who are undeniably good. There are people who want to help. There are people still fighting to make the world a better place. Through our contact, I've seen a side to Iraq that few others will ever get to know—the loving, loyal, and compassionate citizens who are trying to rise above the rubble of their destroyed landscape. As I try to come to terms with my brother's death and find some peace, I realize that our battles are more intertwined than I had previously thought.

That we are all praying for rebirth.

Clearance

There are people who move smoothly between worlds, who seem born to politick and bound across all sorts of borders. They never seem uncomfortable, and they seem to know everyone. I am not one of those people. Growing up in a small town and being very close to my family, I never had to spend much time outside of that circle. That's not to say that my life has been comfortable—I look back on my journey as a single mother and on getting my master's in social work, and I understand that I'm able to get outside of my comfort zone. The past few weeks of talking to total strangers on the other side of the world has given me a little confidence, but I'm a long way from being some kind of jet-setting diplomat.

I know that we're at the point, now, where we need someone with those kinds of connections. Specifically, someone who has the ability to interact with the military in an official capacity. It's something that many Americans take for granted, but as I am clicking through lists of representatives on Michigan's state government website, I am so thankful for our democracy and the people in it who are responsive and responsible for us. I think of Aymen and his family in Iraq. There's no official he can e-mail to ask for help.

My family and I write letters to Governor Jennifer Granholm explaining our situation. With all the press surrounding Peter's passing and the story of the dogs, she's already familiar with what we're trying to do. She points us toward our United States Senator, Carl Levin. Starting from his general website, we find addresses to send our letters of appeal, explaining our story.

People love to complain about the slow crawl of bureaucracy, and sometimes I have to admit it's warranted. But not in our case. It's not long before Carl Levin's assistant, Justin Harlem, writes to us to say that Senator Levin wants to throw whatever support he can our way. In fact, Justin explains, Senator Levin has served on committees that handle some of the decision-making with the Defense Department during wartime, and so he has connections that will be of particular use to us as far as the military is concerned.

Through Senator Levin and Governor Granholm, we are able to get letters sent to the commanding officers of Peter's unit in Iraq asking them to at the very least turn a blind eye to what was about to happen. We would need the soldiers' help in getting the dogs off the base, and even though this might be against military policy, Senator Levin and Governor Granholm pleaded with the military to let this slide.

Senator Levin and Justin Harlem are particularly crucial when it comes to navigating the logistical nightmare of security checkpoints. They tell us that if we are successful in getting the dogs, there will still be twelve security checkpoints standing between the base and getting out of Iraqi airspace. Whoever is going to move the dogs through those checkpoints will need prior clearance from the Army. In peacetime, this would be nearly impossible. In wartime? It is out of the question.

Justin and Senator Levin let us know they won't be taking no for an answer, however, and we once again find ourselves in the position of having to ignore the big red flashing warning signs in front of us: "Don't get your hopes up. This is too hard." I cling to Peter's memory, and I push them out of the way, and soon, another door slowly starts to creak open.

Senator Levin has secured clearance for a private defense contractor, Threat Management Group Agility Logistics (TMG), to be the ones to shepherd the dogs from the base through the Green Zone and onto the plane. They will also have to administer the vaccines to the dogs, since the Murrani family can not get clearance from the military to approach the base. It isn't that the military doesn't trust us or them, Senator Levin explains, it's just that it isn't fair to ask them to trust anyone. I definitely understand, and it is a little easier to swallow this knowing that another piece of the puzzle has fallen into place with TMG. My confidence is bolstered by the fact that John Wagner of Gryphon Airlines has worked with TMG before and sends me his wholehearted support for their involvement in the operation.

After Justin Harlem and Senator Levin make contact with TMG, it's not long after that I get a call from Gerard Righetti, one of the owners of TMG. The line crackles as Gerard's voice comes on, reaching out to me all the way from Australia, where the company is headquartered. He lets me know that his company will gladly volunteer their services for the unusual mission. I exhale, the dollar signs that had been mounting up in front of my eyes flying off into the ether, from whence these gracious souls keep coming.

Gerard and I discuss the security checkpoints and other obstacles that could crop up while transporting the dogs from the base to the airplane. He assures me that he'll contact his top man in Iraq, Peter Ransby, who is the country manager for TMG there, to make all the necessary arrangements. Through e-mails and occasional phone calls, Peter works out the timing and logistics with me, dealing with every single roadblock that pops up. We eventually get things set up and timed so that we'll have the Murrani's ready and waiting at a certain point when they can get clearance to meet up with TMG to go over the paperwork and vaccinations before moving on to the airport to meet Rich Crook, who will be flown in by Gryphon Airlines. Even though some of the clearances have already been secured, there is a constant undertone of security issues: The military lets us know through Senator Levin's office that Rich will not be allowed off the Gryphon plane, not even to step one foot onto the tarmac. It continues to be clear what a mountain we are still going to have to climb. In every moment, there are forks in the road where things could go south. But with the Murranis, Rich Crook, John Wagner, and now friends in high places in the U.S. government as well as TMG on our side, the battle begins to look less and less like a David-and-Goliath kind of affair.

★ ★ ★

The day is January 11, 2008. Peter has been dead for eighteen days, and today is his birthday. He would have been 29.

Although I was born on the 13th, Peter and I always celebrated our birthdays together growing up, trading off days or having our party in between the two. We always shared the same birthday cake and opened presents at the same time. We shared birthday parties. Even later, when his tours with the military conspired to keep us apart, we would always talk on the phone or make some type of contact. I had joked with him when he was home on leave that October that I wasn't going to age again until another year came and we could celebrate our birthday together. "That's fine with me," he assured me, "we can just wait until I'm home again. We just won't count the years that I have to be away."

As with the other plans we made that night, things have changed. This will be the first year since he was born that we won't be celebrating our birthdays together. For me, instead of an occasion of celebration, it is another crushing reminder about the long stretch of time ahead of me that is waiting—a life without Peter.

I try to explain to everyone as best I can that I'll be following the continuous e-mail and phone loops tomorrow, but for today, I need to be out of touch. I need to mourn again. I spend a lot of time that day by myself, after Patrick has gone off to school—lying in bed and staring at the ceiling, walking around the neighborhood, driving in my car. Thinking about Peter, remembering our lives together. His death is somehow still not 100 percent real for me, not even after seeing his body in the funeral home and attending the service. But for some reason, being so irrevocably apart from him on his birthday makes it a little more real.

At the end of the day, after I've made dinner for Patrick and me and he's done his homework and is getting ready for bed, I return to my room to check in to see what I've missed on the e-mail carousel from the day. Things are still moving in a stutter-stop way; we will roll the ball forward, then backward. It's complicated by the dogs themselves, who can't always be located. There are questions of timing and flight conditions, and even though we have the clearances for TMG, there still needs to be the perfect window to line up between them and the men on Peter's base. It can happen at any moment, which makes it also feel like it might never happen. My phone is always on; ready to receive the news at the drop of a hat. In Utah, Rich is ready to take off with Gryphon whenever the word comes down.

One of the e-mails I click is an article sent to me by a friend. I open it and read about the first snow in Baghdad to fall in over a century. My eyes well up with tears, blurring the text on the screen. I know that this has to be a message from Peter. Peter, who always loved the snow, who loved to run and play in it with me when we were kids and even when we were no longer young, just young at heart. Reading the article makes me feel like Peter is still with me, still communicating, still helping move the mission along. Like he

knew what was going on, how hard we were fighting to get his dogs home. He was doing all he could
to help us, and on his birthday, he still gave us all a
present—those improbable, downy flakes that rained
down over the desert that day.

SIXTEEN

Resting in Peace

There are awful things—incomprehensible things—that you may have to live with.

You may have to live with heartbreak, with loss. You may have to bury your brother or son, your husband or wife. You may have to cleave your life in two worlds, separated as if by lightning strike, the before and ever-after. You may have to face the rest of time, all the tragedies and triumphs, feeling completely and utterly alone. You feel phantom pains, like after the loss of a limb—they shoot deep into your heart, agitating you, keeping you up at night, making you the keeper of a constant ghost.

While this all happens, you think that you couldn't possibly be dealt any further blows. That the universe will only give you what you can handle, and you can't handle this, so this must be it.

You are wrong.

I know this because we still have not been able to

lay Peter to rest, now weeks into January. While his body has been cremated and is now long gone—my last memories of him are of my fixing his hair before saying a final good-bye at the funeral home—his organs have been shuttled from lab to lab. First, it was the military's medical examiner's office in Dover, Delaware, where his heart, his brains, and kidneys remained behind while they conducted the autopsy to try to determine the cause of his death, still shrouded in mystery.

The harsh reality of this as I was having that moment with Peter at the funeral home was heartbreaking. I still grit my teeth at the memory of the funeral attendant reminding me to be careful with his head, not wanting to disturb whatever delicate lie they had made to cover up his missing brain. It was weeks ago, and still, it makes me feel as though the air has been knocked out of me. The thought of Peter's organs being taken from him and sitting in some lab somewhere is so far beyond what I would ever expect to have to think about, even after opening the door on Christmas Day and hearing what I heard.

While we are busy trying to get safe passage for Mama and Boris, the military continues to conduct tests on Peter's remains until they are satisfied that they've come up with all the information they can. Unfortunately, the tests have yet to shed light on anything. His organs are normal, healthy—his heart is vital, there is no reason they can find for it to have stopped beating. They let us know that at the moment, they have no further answers, and they might not for quite some time. With what knowledge of healthcare I have, I am suspicious of what I've heard in bits and pieces. I demand to see the results of the blood work, not understanding how these questions have not been answered. When the organs are released, we arrange to pay for a private examination. We trust the Army, but whatever the cause of Peter's death, we want to be sure, even if it means going through heartbreak all over again. Even if it means delaying putting him to rest.

I can almost feel him in the space above my head in each room, in the air, in every draft that blows through my house. He is not at peace, not yet. Of course, neither are we.

It is the end of January when we can finally cremate Peter's organs and combine them with the rest of his ashes in one urn. The finality of it brings with it some sense of relief: That business is done, and we can maybe move on from here. It's wishful thinking, I know. But wishes are all I have to hang on to.

Peter had talked about wanting to be cremated, in the sort of offhand way that people do when they talk about their future plans, but he was only in his late twenties; we had never discussed any type of real burial plans. Our family is torn between two places:

Peter's favorite place in the world, the Upper Peninsula where our family hunting camp is, and anywhere
closer to us. We are still reeling from the loss, and the
thought of scattering his remains in the Upper Peninsula, hours away, is more than we can bear.

My mother and I take a forty-five minute drive
to the closest national cemetery in Holly, Michigan,
on the suggestion of a casualty assistance officer. We
want to see if it will be a good fit for Peter's final resting place. We are hopeful that it will be, as it's close
enough that we can still go visit.

We drive together in relative silence, apart from
a few words of conversation about what needs to
be done next, what Peter would have wanted; we're
still very task-oriented at this point, and numb to the
world. The car falls quiet as we pull off the freeway
and take in the scenery, which is eerily reminiscent of
the drives to the Upper Peninsula and our cottage in
Caseville. The landscape echoes so many family vacations and happier times.

We pull into the cemetery and immediately feel
at ease, and in awe. It is beautiful, and so peaceful,
and somehow it feels right to us. Fieldstone walls line
the main road, marked by a cadre of proud American
flags, recalling the storied scape of Arlington National
Cemetery. The property is surrounded by woods and
a glistening lake; birds and other animals are the only
sounds to be heard for what seems like miles. Instantly,

we know: Here, we will be able to visit him whenever we want—so it is with the hope that neither he, nor we, will ever be fully alone that we reserve a vault at Great Lakes National Cemetery where his ashes will be interred.

When we make this decision, my father takes the clipping of hair that he'd taken from Peter's body before he was cremated and takes it up north, where he has a boulder carved with his name and an inscription—"Home is the hunter"—inspired by a piece of poetry by Robert Louis Stevenson. In the poem, Stevenson's narrator lays out his wishes for when he passes on; he wants to be buried under the beautiful skies and open heavens where he felt most alive:

> *Under the wide and starry sky,*
> *Dig the grave and let me lie:*
> *Glad did I live and gladly die.*
> *And I laid me down with a will.*
> *This be the verse you 'grave for me:*
> *Here he lies where he longed to be;*
> *Home is the sailor, home from the sea,*
> *and the hunter home from the hill.*

With the lock of hair, the boulder and the inscription, my father has made a perfect memorial for Peter there, so that Peter's spirit can always return to his favorite spot. The boulder sits right where Peter and I did that night in the woods, alongside two beer cans that we left behind, unopened, that stand as a light-hearted reminder of our last night, our promises, our companionship, and the hope we had for the future. As my father describes the scene to us, I say a prayer that one day, I can have that hope again.

On January 30, 2008, we hold an interment ceremony for our immediate family and a couple of our closest aunts, uncles, and cousins. We hold another memorial service, this one more intimate and personal. Both the Honor Guard and Patriot Riders show up again, flanking the ceremony. My father and I both speak again, and while I may have been able to keep from falling to pieces at the public service, there is no such luck this time. I sob my way through two poems and have a hard time standing up. Outside, the wind howls in near-blizzard conditions, the world seemingly falling down around us.

When we get to the interment wall, one of the staff members tells us that this is where Peter's final resting place will be, and that we can put anything we would like inside the vault with his ashes. There is a momentary reprieve from my tears as my body is wracked with anger instead; we are completely unprepared for this option—nobody had mentioned it before. "How can you not tell us something like that?" I scream at the casualty assistance officer, who looks just as taken aback as I am. There is no calming me down once I've started to wind up, until cooler heads prevail and we see what we have on our persons that we can leave with Peter to remind him of us for the rest of time.

My mom takes off her ring, which bears the Celtic symbol for everlasting love. I remove my necklace, which had another Celtic symbol for infinity—the circle of life and three points that connect the life now with the life thereafter. We have some pictures of our family with us that we place in the vault along with the jewelry, as well as pictures of Mama and Boris. That will have to be enough, I think. Everyone reassures me that it is perfect, everything worked out perfectly, and I stare at the internment wall in the bitter cold and think that perfection is a hard sell for me right now.

Just as they are sealing the vault, my phone rings. I look down. I've left it on because the situation with Mama and Boris has reached a point of any-minute-now urgency, and I want to be available at all hours of the day to answer any questions and give any assistance that I can. The number on the screen is Rich Crook's.

"I'm sorry," I say to my family, huddled by the wall in a circle, tears in their eyes. "I have to take this."

I step outside the circle and put a hand up to my ear so that I can hear every word of Rich's call clearly. "You're not going to believe this, Carey," he says, "but it's all come together."

"What?" I'm having trouble processing anything at the moment.

"It's happening. I'm leaving on a plane in a couple of days for Baghdad. Everything is a go."

A sob catches in my throat. "We're bringing them home, Carey."

I can't speak. I click off the phone and fall to my knees. My family rushes to my side, worried at first that something terrible has happened. But soon, I'm able to tell them the good news. I look at the sealed vault where Peter is finally resting in peace, and I thank him over and over. Because now I know he is still watching, he is still here, and still helping us.

Mama and Boris are coming home.

SEVENTEEN

The Journey Home

The reports start to trickle in from Baghdad in a string of short phone calls, e-mails, and photo attachments. Because I can't be there, I'm crawling out of my skin—I'm worried about what might go wrong, I'm worried about complications I haven't even thought of yet. I spend a lot of time pacing my house and yard, hoping that Peter's spirit can help where my hands are tied.

Rich Crook is up in the air over the Middle East, where it is the middle of the night. A brief stopover in Kuwait turns into a couple days of layover while TMG makes last-minute adjustments on the ground in Baghdad. He is given shelter by the PAWS rescue organization, and puts up with my frantic phone calls day and night. He is ever the cheerleader, ever the calming, positive presence. "We're going to get this done, Carey. It's happening."

While Rich stands at the ready in Kuwait, TMG

tries to wrangle both of the dogs. I almost have a heart attack when Peter from TMG calls me to tell me that his men were only able to retrieve Mama from the base and get her to a secure location. When they went to find the dogs to administer the vaccines, the puppy was nowhere to be found.

Immediately, all rational thought flies from my mind. Of course I know the incredible dangers that these men are facing and the seemingly limitless generosity they are displaying for me, a stranger they'd not be able to pick out in a crowd. They owe me nothing, and I owe them everything. But I am not thinking about that as I cry and beg Peter to go back and get the puppy. "Please. You can't leave him there. Please go back."

For some reason, Peter relents, and I try to pull myself together to thank him. The TMG team goes back once again, across the desert and through all sorts of dangers clear and unseen. Thankfully no one is hurt, and they are able to retrieve Boris. They send me pictures: Tough men clad in body armor, their eyes obscured by mirrored sunglasses, smiling and laughing as they play with the dogs, walking them around with leashes and collars they've made out of rope. I can see the effects that these dogs have on even the most experienced soldiers, their unbidden joy jumping out from the photos. CEO Gerard Righetti checks in, too, e-mailing with the touching, supportive update that he's been keeping his young daughter apprised of the mission as a hopeful bedtime story. I know how badly he wants to give her a story with a happy ending, and it makes me feel better to know that this man is on my side.

The call comes in the middle of the night from TMG to Gryphon to get Rich on the plane. All at once sleepy and pumped full of adrenaline, Rich flies up over the mountains and through the darkness on a Gryphon plane sidelined by two military escort aircraft. The plane keeps to high altitudes to avoid missile fire, and the only light that comes through the small windows is from the softly blinking markers on the wings of the escorts.

A crackly voice comes on over the intercom to tell Rich: "Hold on tight. We're going down." The plane takes a nosedive into the Baghdad airport, not risking flying in low. All of the lights on the plane turn out, and they plummet toward the ground. Rich tells me later about the eerie sight of the airport: While we're used to a million lights guiding the way from the runway to the gate, at the Baghdad airport, they are plunged into total darkness. It is another world away, in the realm of military maneuvers, stealth and studied deception.

The sun has not yet started to peek over the unfeeling steppes of the Iraqi highlands when the TMG team appears from the darkness, efficiently delivering

Mama and Boris to the plane. The whole operation takes about twenty minutes, and the men disappear back into the unbroken dawn in silence as the plane takes off—with no lights on—and begins the return journey to Kuwait.

Once they are in the air, Rich is able to let the dogs out of their crates and give them food and water and see how they are doing. Mama and Boris are in rough shape. Both animals are dehydrated, emaciated, and covered in welts and bald patches from a scabies infection. Afterward, Rich admits to us that he was afraid they wouldn't survive the trip to America. He says without hesitation that if they had spent even a few more days in Baghdad, they would have been done for, gone forever like Peter.

Once in Kuwait, Rich transfers with the dogs to a commercial airline, where they must be put in the cargo hold. It's dark down there, and the dogs are already considerably traumatized by the flight, but Rich has no choice but to comply with the regulations— the dogs are way too big to fly with the passengers. He accompanies them into the hold, where it's cold and loud, the roaring of the engines shaking the floor. He makes sure they are as comfortable as possible, loading their crates up with blankets to keep them warm and coaxing them to drink as much water as possible. He tells me he is worried sick that they won't make it to Washington, D.C. Up in the passenger cabin, Rich doesn't sleep a wink on the long journey—he stares out the window and hopes against hope that the dogs can hang on just a little longer.

Once the plane lands at Dulles Airport in D.C., Rich goes down to the cargo hold to see the dogs, who are blessedly still breathing. They are met at the gate by Senator Levin's assistant, Justin Harlem, who is there to help us clear another hurdle. Normally, the Centers for Disease Control requires a thirty-day quarantine for any animals coming into the United States. But Rich has made it clear to Justin that this won't be an option. Justin explains the situation to the CDC, and based on our promises and his affidavit that we will keep them in a home quarantine for thirty days, they are allowed to go on to Michigan as an exception.

Like everyone else who meets the dogs, Justin is immediately touched by their spirit. He brings toys and treats for them, and kneels down on the pavement to greet them. They take to him immediately and get a few last bits of love from one of their many guardian angels before they join Rich and Best Friends photographer Molly Wald for the final leg of their journey.

The dogs have acclimated to Rich during their long journey, but Molly and Rich are both surprised by how quickly they accept new people. They bond with Molly instantly, trusting her implicitly as they have done with the men from TMG, Rich, and Justin.

Every person these dogs come into contact with sees what Peter saw—how special and loving and healing they are. It's clear from their demeanor how much time Peter spent socializing them and getting them comfortable with human touch—for feral street dogs from Baghdad, they are both trusting, wriggly love bugs.

"I've never seen rescue dogs adjust to new people so quickly," Rich tells me, and I think about how it's a testament to all the love they've been shown in their short, often difficult lives. These dogs are now on a journey of love: Not just because of Peter, or the people they will meet over the next few days—but also because of hundreds of men and women they'll never know who gave all that they could: their time, their money, their thoughts and prayers. Their lives are miraculous.

"How are they doing so far?" I ask.

"They're taking it all in stride," he says. "I don't know, it's strange. It's almost as if this was something they were expecting."

Molly and Rich herd the dogs into a van, and they take off to the north. As they reach the northern border of Pennsylvania, they stop for the night at a Motel 6, where Rich brings them inside. He calls me on the phone and describes the incredible sight to me, and I can hear their excited barking in the background. The dogs have never been inside a building before, let alone a motel. They explore the whole room: Boris bounds up onto the bedspread while Mama sniffs the corners; they roll around on the carpet; they look quizzically at the television; they are warm and comfortable. Molly and Rich look on with concern as they both scratch and claw at the raw wounds all over their bodies, and wrangle them into the tub to give them their first bath. Rich e-mails me adorable pictures of the furry mongrels, covered in medicated soap and tongues lolling out, splashing water all over Rich and Molly.

When the dogs are all dry and ready for bed, Rich clicks off the lights, and each pup curls up on the soft carpet, a feeling unlike anything they've ever felt before.

I wonder if they know where they're heading.

EIGHTEEN

Welcome Home, Mama and Boris

It is the morning of February 8, and our whole family is one raw bundle of nerves—me more so than the rest. That morning, I hang up the red, white, and blue banner on the front of our house. I tie up the balloons—also red, white, and blue—that I've bought for the homecoming. I take a step back into the yard to take in the view. Then I close my eyes, thinking about another homecoming that I can only imagine.

The homecoming takes place on July 4, Independence Day. The air smells like smoky hamburgers and sunscreen, all of those American summertime smells. The sun is bright; the sky is clear; and there is no rain in the forecast. I stand in the yard in front of another set of balloons, another banner. I pace back and forth, putting a rut in the grass. Kids roll down the street on their skateboards and razor scooters and tricycles;

Patrick roars up and down the driveway on a Big Wheel. My mom is inside, putting icing on a cake that has finally cooled. Peter will be home any moment now.

When I open my eyes, it is cold and gray, with a light blanket of frost coating the lawn. The banner hung proudly over the front door reads Welcome Home, Mama and Boris. The balloons are for them, not Peter. It's not the homecoming I had planned, I think as I shiver, hop from foot to foot, try to keep from tearing up on what should be a joyful morning. I shake off my sadness like I shake off the cold, and I go back inside.

Rich calls to let us know that he should be there, precious cargo in tow, sometime in the late afternoon. I hang up the phone and try to focus on something, anything but the hours that stand between us and this long-anticipated moment. I pick up a magazine, listlessly thumb through a couple pages, and throw it back down on the coffee table. I straighten up things around the house, dusting the same spots over and over again, as if I'm preparing for the scrutiny of a health inspection. It's not long before I make the decision to go into work. If I stay here, I think, I will spontaneously combust, my innards exploding all over the living room. My mother would not appreciate this, I decide, and I take off to make myself useful for the day.

I spend the morning talking to clients, checking

in on hospice patients, filling out paperwork. I try to keep my eyes from wandering to check the time. Suddenly, there are clock faces everywhere: daunting analog tickers like you'd look to during the last minutes of the school day, blinking digital numbers on microwaves, and on and on. It feels like an eternity is crawling by instead of an ordinary workday. Finally, enough grains of sand have dropped through today's timer that I feel comfortable returning home to make the final preparations for our guests of honor.

As I turn onto our normally quiet street, I'm greeted by lines of television trucks and crowds of reporters. Throngs of people stand in our front yard, craning their necks to see who is going to get out of the car. They almost seemed disappointed when they see that it is just me and that the dogs—the stars of the show—are not in tow.

"Carey! Carey!" they clamor, and I'm having the surreal moment of understanding what life must be like for a celebrity, no matter how minor. "When are Mama and Boris getting here?"

I look around, floored by the number of people crowding our lawn and spilling out into the street. I see neighbors trying to get to their driveways, only to be thwarted by the news vans. A generally unassuming person, I feel embarrassed and self-conscious at the idea that I'm inconveniencing my whole block. My ears redden as I try to plaster on a smile, and I know

I must look dazed in all the photos they are taking, since I am blinded by their camera flashes. Little stars float in front of my eyes. "They're coming soon," I say, blinking and trying to adjust to the scene in front of me. I remember that the PR department of Best Friends had sent out a press release in advance of the homecoming, and I know that the announcement, combined with the hopeful story, has brought on all of this attention.

I desperately want to give in to the impulse to run into the house, lock and barricade the door behind me, and hide until Rich and Molly get here with the dogs. But I know that I owe it to many, many people to make sure that I thank them as properly as I can, and for a lot of those people, that includes mentioning them in the media. Of course, none of them have asked me for any such repayment, but aside from the small financial contributions I've been able to make thanks to the generosity of all those who've sent in donations, it's the only currency I've got. I want to make sure that all the good people who helped us along the way get as much credit as I can possibly give them. They deserve so much more.

I take a deep breath and start inviting the TV cameras and reporters into our house. We cram as many as can possibly fit into our small living room, the boom mics bumping against the ceiling as I hold an ad hoc press conference in front of our fireplace. I answer questions about how I'm feeling, about Peter, about his legacy, and about what the dogs mean to me. I put my hands on Patrick's shoulders and talk about how much Peter meant to our family and, by extension, how much all the people who have helped us mean to our family now, too. And nothing could be more true. In the midst of all this heartbreak, the love in our lives has actually managed to grow.

I thank as many people as I can, and I list even more for the newspaper reporters who agree to take down more notes. My stomach turns with the worry that I have forgotten someone; there are so many people to thank—maybe even more than I realize. I thank John Wagner at Gryphon, Senator Levin and Governor Granholm, TMG, the Army, the soldiers of Peter's company. I thank the Murranis, although they may never see the broadcast. I thank Best Friends. I thank the media, too, for all of the coverage they have given us—coverage that resulted in thousands of e-mails from helpful strangers. "These people have taken an impossible situation and made it possible. And I will never be able to repay them for what they've done," I say, getting a bit choked up. "A million dollars wouldn't repay them for what they did. So you need to know that these people exist. And that they're angels."

When Rich calls to let me know that they are about twenty minutes away, I politely ask the media if they would mind if I stopped interviewing. I can see that they're reticent; not everyone has gotten the chance to get a unique sound bite. But they respect my wishes and clear out. I feel bad, looking at the snow and cold winds swirling outside, but I know that our family needs a couple of minutes to regroup. My mom reminds me that they have vans to take shelter in if they need to. I smile at her, appreciating that she understands what many others on hand today don't— how the sadness of this occasion is inextricably linked to our happiness.

Most reporters and onlookers stay out on the lawn though, looking down the road, hoping to see that van crest over the horizon. While we wait, I try to take the time to sit quietly and do some deep breathing, hoping that it will help keep me from falling to pieces when the dogs arrive.

In the room with me are my Aunt Julie and cousin Sarah, two of the family members who had been most involved in the rescue process. We are also joined by my mother and her other two sisters, all eager to see our dream come to fruition. I explain to Patrick that along with the dogs, the ABC *World News* team is also in the van with their cameras, documenting the journey, and they'd need to come in to the house too in order to take some pictures. He can barely contain his excitement—although he's grown up around dogs and cats, he's never had any to call his own. Mama and Boris will be his dogs, dogs whose affections he has

seem to be. "I've rescued a lot of strays from crazy situations, Carey, and I have never seen anything like this," he says.

Mama hops onto the couch and starts licking her paws. Boris joins her and gets settled in on a pillow. Rich looks on, shaking his head in disbelief. "It's as if I were bringing your own dogs back to you," he says, marveling at the mystery.

To me, it's no mystery at all. They are Peter's dogs, and they know it. They know that Peter has been here, that we try to keep him alive in spirit. This was his home, and this will be their home now. They know that we are supposed to be together, and although it's not the homecoming we had planned, it is amazing in its own way.

After a last interview with ABC *World News,* the news teams pull out. Life returns to normal on our little snow-laced street. We open the door and go back into the cold, in the backyard this time, just us, Rich and Molly, and our new best friends. We light the grill and have a small barbecue, eating hamburgers in hands clad in woolen mittens. We laugh and cry, hug each other, watch the dogs play in the yard where they will live, happy and healthy, safe and sound.

It's nothing like I imagined it: It is not July. Peter is not here. But now, only now, he is finally home.

NINETEEN

A New Life

Rich and Molly stay in Michigan for a few days, helping to get the dogs adjusted. I'm so glad they've decided to stick around. Although we've only known each other for a little over a month, there is no question that we've made a very deep, lifelong bond. We spend hours sitting on the living room couch with the dogs, watching them chew on the toys that Justin Harlem gave them back at Dulles, laugh at them when they fall asleep by the fire and start to snore, and just generally revel in being near them without any obstacles to keep us apart. Rich tells us stories of some of the rescues he's organized in the most havoc-ridden disaster zones; Molly shows us the beautiful pictures she's taken from Mama and Boris's first road trip.

After everyone has recuperated from their ordeal, Rich and Molly help us begin training and housebreaking. We've had dogs before, but never dogs who have spent their first years literally running wild, so it's a little difficult at first. How do you tell creatures who have known only the boundary of the horizon that they must stay in one place and do their business in another? The answer is, of course, not easily. We are so grateful that they're here, though, that it's not hard to have patience with them. Every morning is like a new life for them, and for me. We wake up and say hello again, and it's like that first day in our driveway. There is so much love, pure and uncomplicated by any of the things that drag down human relationships. There is truly nothing to be ambivalent about with them; when we look at them, we feel only happiness.

The media still stick around on the fringes of our daily routine; I answer a few more phone calls from the local papers and even do an interview on NPR. It's pretty incredible that two stray dogs from Baghdad could pull at the heartstrings of an entire nation and stay in the spotlight for a few months. But for the most part, things are starting to calm down and get back to normal, or at least our new normal.

The dogs' presence in our lives continues to invite kindness from the community. Cards and care packages with toys and treats keep coming in the mail—an endless Christmas for Mama and Boris—from strangers who have been touched by the story and wanted to send a little something. Banfield Pet Hospital donates an entire year of veterinary care for both dogs, so we will be able to get all of the shots that they'll need and follow-up checkups without having to pay anything. As they get stronger, my heart sings every morning when I wake up to see that their coats were improving, getting less patchy, shinier. And at night, when I get home from work, when I am greeted by their wagging tails, I am able to forget about everything for a moment—all the sadness of the past few months is blocked out as Mama and Boris show me how happy they are to see me.

There are still struggles, little ones that any dog owner can attest to. Of course, Mama and Boris have their own unique issues to deal with. One is that after a lifetime of eating scraps, garbage, MREs, and whatever they could find or beg from the soldiers, their stomachs are not accustomed to dog food. It takes a long while before I can get them to even approach a bowl; Mama in particular gives me a sassy face, as if to ask me what I am trying to pull on her. Once I am able to trick them into eating some of the kibble by mixing in rice, chicken, or beef and coaxing them to the dish, it isn't long before unpleasant explosions dot our rugs and floors. They watch me as I scoop their poop from every imaginable corner and crevice—I think at first it is out of concern and curiosity, but after getting to know the mischievous devils a little better, I question whether they aren't trying to tell me I told you so.

We also are very concerned that they'll try to run

off. After living in the streets of Baghdad barely contained, it makes sense that they'd want to wander. We
have a big fenced-in yard for them to play in, but I
know how smart they are; after all, Mama broke into
a base that government-approved defense contractors
had to spend weeks getting clearance to enter. I am
sick with worry, much like I was for the first few years
of Patrick's life—turning on the lights after they've
fallen asleep to check and double check that they are
still there. New motherhood makes you crazy. I am
so grateful when we get a call from an invisible fence
company, who donates an entire invisible fence system, as well as free monitoring for a year.

Training and socialization continue to be a bit of
a sticking point—not with people, whom they love
almost on sight—but with other dogs. Suddenly, our
neighborhood seems to have more dogs per capita
than any other in the world. Taking Mama and Boris
for a walk is a dicey proposition; I learn to see dogs
coming out of the corner of my eye, and it starts to
feel like an arcade game where I'm dodging obstacles
and prone to false starts. We put on the leashes and get
going, only to see one of their neighborhood nemeses
padding down the sidewalk. Their protective, territo-
rial instincts are understandable, and I chalk it up to
the life they've led so far. It's easy to overlook when
we're safe in our living room; they watch over Patrick and me like benevolent hawks, and I know how

gentle they truly are. But I don't expect my neighbors to understand if it's their beloved pooch involved in a turf scuffle.

Luckily for us, our scruffy new additions are universally loved darlings with a worldwide reputation! Joel Silverman from Animal Planet's "Good Dog U" calls up one day and offers to come out to meet them. I take him up on it immediately, explaining some of the issues we're having. Before I know it, he has camped out at our house for a couple days, helping me with training—simple commands, behavior modification, all things that he is so well versed in. To have a celebrity animal trainer dedicate his time and talents to us is yet another gift we could never repay.

I am able to follow up that training with a few months of work from a local trainer, Jim Lessenberry, who runs Animal Learning Systems. He works very intensely with us on their behavior issues, leash pulling, barking, and housebreaking. And during this time, our bond continues to strengthen. From the first night, Boris has slept in Patrick's bedroom. Now Mama curls up at the foot of the bed, watching over both of her pups—her own and her adopted human. I can tell they feel safe here.

As time passes, we get to know them more, all their little quirks and habits. They both hate baths, rain, and snow—any kind of precipitation feels foreign to them, and they want nothing to do with it. I know that getting them to swim up at the lake in the Upper Peninsula will be an angry, wriggly comedy of errors at best.

Mama's personality is the first to announce itself: she is hyper, intelligent, and extremely manipulative. Sitting under the dinner table, she has normally unwilling guests fawning all over her, their hands constantly reaching down to give her a morsel of whatever she wants. Kibble is still a challenge, but leftovers are delicious, and she knows how to get what she wants. She's also incredibly sensitive and attentive—when I'm sad, she tends to mirror my mood, looking up at me mournfully and snuggling up so that I have some fur to cry into. When I'm happy, she's bouncy and jumpy. When I'm angry, her hackles will go up in a pinch, ready to neutralize any threat to me, real or imagined. She only weighs about forty pounds, but it's quickly clear that she's the queen of the house.

Boris is more laid back, tentative, and unsure. He's growing into a big boy—I think probably he'll top out at around eighty pounds. But that doesn't keep him from being a total scaredy-cat, hiding behind my legs if he feels worried. As he gets older, I can see that he will probably be a puppy for life, all big paws and slobbery kisses. His favorite toy is the tennis ball—I like thinking of Peter when we play fetch now, and hope he's watching us, taking pride that Boris has finally learned how to do it right. I talk to them both about Peter all the time, telling them stories about

him, about how much he loved them. When his belongings finally make their way back to us in a box, I
take out a shirt of his and give it to them. They wag
their tails as I dangle it in front of them, and they take
it and curl up with it immediately, breathing in his
scent and remembering him, just as I do every time I
hear a certain song or see a particularly beautiful sunrise. To me, they are so clearly his children. It doesn't
matter if they're covered in fur—they represent the
same bright future that my unborn nieces and neph-
ews would have.

To have them home is the most incredible feeling
in the world. I've rescued other dogs before, but this
experience brings that feeling to an entirely new level.
It starts to sink in: all that we've been able to accomplish, the miracle of their journey, the friends we've
made along the way. They are a reminder of Peter's
life and how he lived it—of how compassionate and
caring he was. When Boris nuzzles up to me on the
couch and licks my tears away or Mama finds me hiding under a blanket, trying to shut myself off from the
world, their love helps me push through the pain. On
days when I don't want to get out of bed and face my
day, knowing that they still need to be fed and let outside gets my feet on the floor, much like my son does
in this bleak world without Peter in it. Then, one foot
in front of the other, I go downstairs, watch them eat,
and give them their medicine. It's not too long before

I find myself thinking that it wouldn't be so bad to have some coffee and go outside. Then, I think that it wouldn't be so bad to go to work.

It wouldn't be so bad to be happy for a while, I think, opening the door and watching them rumble around the yard. Right now, this moment, I can be happy. Looking at those wagging tails, those floppy paws seeming to launch them into flight, I think I just might be. Happy.

★ ★ ★

Winter creeps slowly on. With each new day comes the uneasy knowledge that what would have been Peter's true homecoming date is fast approaching. We are still clamoring for answers from the Army, which is continuing its investigation into Peter's death. It is sometimes hard to focus on moving forward.

We receive an invitation to come down to Fort Stewart in Georgia, where Peter's infantry division is based. There is to be a tree planting ceremony on Warrior's Walk, something that the 3rd Infantry Division does periodically for its soldiers who have lost their lives in Iraq and Afghanistan. Peter's tree is scheduled to be planted at the end of February, alongside trees for six other fallen soldiers.

My family goes down in two separate cars, my mother and Patrick and I traveling down together in one. We make the decision to stop and stay in Hilton Head, where we always went on family vacations as children and then again after Patrick's birth. There, on the grassy shores of the Outer Banks, Peter and I would play in the surf, making sandcastles and eating ice cream, our faces sticky with sprinkles and chocolate.

Though it's windy and gray, I take a walk along the beach when we get there. I know that this is where Peter spent his last weekend before deployment, where he and his friends had a last hurrah. It was such a special place for him, and being here feels comforting in some ways and painful in others, much like anything that reminds me of him. Out in the soft breaking of the waves, I can see us long ago, back before it all changed. I wrap my coat around me tightly and walk back, joining my family at the hotel to get some sleep, or at least try to, before the next day dawns.

Down in Fort Stewart, we make our way to Warrior's Walk, where we are greeted by a plaque celebrating the soldiers commemorated here by the hundreds of Eastern Redbud trees, some stretching strongly toward the sky, others just starting out, those losses still fresh, those families still reeling. The plaque says:

> *This is where they are welcomed when they return home from battle. It is this field where warriors walk. And it is here on this walkway that we remember our courageous soldiers who demonstrated*

exceptional valor, honor and respect for their Army, their country and their belief in their cause during Operations Iraqi Freedom and Enduring Freedom. The Eastern Redbud trees along the walkway are a symbol of life and will be a living tribute to the brave soldiers who paid the ultimate price for our freedom.

A living tribute, I think, is a beautiful thing. That is something I can get behind, even in all my grief. I think of Mama and Boris, those beating, beautiful hearts. Living tributes.

The ceremony is brief but emotional. Kristopher, the soldier who accompanied Peter's body from Iraq back to Dover and then Michigan, made sure that he was assigned to accompany our family at the ceremony. I'm embarrassed when I don't recognize him, and touched that he would want to follow us through the process, offering the comfort that he could. The men leading the dedication read a few short paragraphs about each soldier and place the plaque in the tree. I had written the part about Peter myself, but hearing it makes me feel hollow, another punch to the stomach—this is real, Peter is gone. Afterward, we place the things we've brought to adorn the branches of Peter's fledgling tree: another necklace symbolizing eternal life from me, a small toy airplane from Patrick, stuffed dogs resembling Mama and Boris from my father and stepmother, Ann. We walk around and look at each of the trees, living monuments to each soldier, much more meaningful than any slab of carved marble. There are small memorial gifts hanging from all of the branches, now bare in the cold final stretch of winter.

★ ★ ★

Shortly after Peter's unit returns in the summer, I make plans with the soldiers that I've been in touch with to come down and visit them, briefly reuniting them with the dogs that they went out of their way to save. Before Peter died, I had never realized what a support system I had in the Army—but now, every day, it grows clearer and clearer. We continue to follow the lives of these soldiers as we would have followed Peter's, celebrating their marriages, the births of their children, and their accomplishments. I want them to know that I am there for them as they have been there for me, so my cousin Sarah and I plan a trip back down south, renting a house in Hilton Head where we camp out with the dogs. We let the soldiers know that anyone who wants to come out is always welcome, and we spend many nights having food and beer, celebrating and remembering Peter and the times we had together.

We take the dogs to Warrior's Walk to visit Peter's tree, and then we take them to the base, where we visit with the unit. They present us with a huge portrait that an Iraqi interpreter painted in memory of Peter, and though our minds boggle at the sheer size of the thing, we still manage to fit it in the van for the trip back home.

While on base, the soldiers all hug the dogs and play fetch with Boris. They marvel at how much the puppy has grown, and at how calm and happy Mama seems. I take a walk around a trailer to look at the painting where it's propped up, and I'm stopped in my tracks by a soldier I've never seen before. "I know you," he says, his eyes sure of something I know not to be true.

"I'm sorry, I don't think we've met."

"But I know you."

Then, suddenly, he bursts into tears. "You're Peter's sister."

Peter and I look so much alike, he thought he saw Peter standing there, proud in his uniform—just for a moment. After Peter's image melts away, he grabs me and hugs me tight, not letting me go for a long time. "Are Mama and Boris here?" he asks, hopeful. I am so happy to show him to them.

The whole weekend is hard to take in, of course, but it is also life-affirming. To see these men who have been through so much, have seen horrible things, and made unimaginable sacrifices, be able to take solace in these dogs is another miracle. To have them home was Peter's dying wish, and together, we were able to fulfill that. Mission accomplished.

★ ★ ★

Over the next two years, we settle into a quiet sort of life at home. Patrick is growing up right alongside Boris, and Mama and I look on proudly. I continue to use Mama and Boris's presence as a foothold for dealing with Peter's loss, desperately searching for the closure that the various memorials and incomplete autopsy reports have not given me. My other focus is maintaining the connections that the whole experience has given to me: my friendships with Rich Crook and his wife Pam, the Murrani family, and Peter's soldiers—my new army family.

Rich and his wife visit a few times a year. The dogs don't forget about him, no matter how much time passes between visits—when they see him, it's like meeting an old friend, and I can see a different level of excitement than they display for the typical visitor. When he can't come visit for a while, he is constantly checking in by phone or e-mail, and I send him mountains of pictures of the dogs looking happy, well fed, and much loved in their new home.

At some point, I hatch a plan to take a trip down to Utah to give back a little to Best Friends. Rich helps me coordinate a volunteer visit. Two of my longtime friends, Suzie and Carrie, are excited to join me and make a girls' weekend out of it. We all meet up at the airport in Las Vegas and rent a car for the drive to Utah.

As soon as we're out of the glaring Vegas lights, the scenery opens up before us in new and beautiful ways. Painted deserts studded with mountain ranges unfold, and I am in awe of this beautiful country. We laugh and talk nonstop, catching up on the last couple years that life has scattered us around the country and away from each other, Carrie in Arizona and Suzie in Colorado. We reminisce about Peter, whom they were close to as well. It's clear to all of us that it's much more than a long weekend, more than just a road trip.

When we arrive at Angel Canyon, the Best Friends animal sanctuary, it's obvious that Rich has paved our way with instructions to give us the VIP treatment. We get an incredible tour from one of the founders of Best Friends, Faith Moloney, in which we learn all about the history of the organization and the various animals they serve. Faith shows us around the sanctuary, a gorgeous, sandy respite for all kinds of creatures set deep within a desert-like climate. The scenery is rugged, mountainous, serene and in some places, completely untouched by man's hand. Here, animals are given more than a second chance at life: They are given an entirely new set of possibilities.

We spend some time volunteering in Dogtown, a set of play areas and runs where all the rescued dogs make their home. We clean up kennels, wash floors, and help out with feeding and grooming. We are even able to take two dogs out on excursions: A sweet pit bull plays fetch with us in a coral sand dune, and a Rottweiler mix named Karma comes back to our hotel with us for a night after taking a long hike with us and Molly Wald, the photographer who traveled with Rich to bring Mama and Boris home. We kiss Karma, pamper her, and love her up as best we can before returning her to Dogtown the next day. It's all we can do—we have to get going back to our jobs and families—but I love knowing that I have been able to give back, even if in just a small way.

On the way back to the airport to return the car, we stop at Zion National Park and the Grand Canyon. Looking out over the plunging vista, I feel a cleansing spirit wash over me and know that Best Friends has helped me once again, even though I was the volunteer. I feel it in my core: some of the healing, the peace, that on my darker days I think will never come.

★ ★ ★

At the end of 2009, we are visited by another angel: Aymen Murrani.

From the moment we connected at the start of the journey, I knew that Aymen would always have a very special place in my heart. Out of everyone involved in our story, he and his family took on the most personal risk, all without hesitation or condition. I stay connected with them, particularly Aymen and

Saud, whom I e-mail with and talk to on the phone all the time. My family writes letters of support for him when he applies for a student visa and entry into the country, something that is very hard for citizens of Iraq to acquire under the circumstances surrounding the war. His petition is successful, and he eventually lands in Florida, where he stays with a sponsor family and studies at a local university. I think it's so brave of him to come over here all by himself, not knowing a soul, at only eighteen years of age. He reports that he's doing extremely well in school, and I can tell from our communication that his English is getting better. It's no surprise to me that he's excelling, this bright young man that I've never met but know so well—compassionate, kind, wise beyond his years, just like the rest of his family.

When Aymen calls to say that he has some free time and wants to come spend it with us in Michigan, I couldn't be happier. He asks if he can come see us, and probably has to drop the phone when I shout an affirmative into the receiver. My cousin Sarah and her mother, Julie, as well as her stepfather, come to stay with us as well. They were so involved in the communications with Aymen during our mission to bring Mama and Boris back, and are just as eager to finally meet him in person.

To put a face to a name and voice is just as amazing as we'd expected. Throughout all of our struggles on this journey, sometimes it felt like the people we had "met" weren't real at all; rather, they were guardian angels who would disappear into thin air once their job was complete. To be able to give Aymen a hug and share a room with him, to watch his bright eyes twinkle as he sat on the floor and held the dogs, was the most incredible feeling. He laughs as I squeeze him until his breath goes out, after which he says: "That's the most sincere hug I've ever gotten in my life."

Aymen is at ease with us immediately, and we spend a few days celebrating his place in our lives. We go out to dinner, spend long nights talking until the wee hours, and take pictures of him and the dogs to send back to his family. When it's time for him to leave, I wish I could roll back the clock and get just a few more hours with him—but I know that no matter how far we are from one another or how long it is until we meet again, we'll be able to pick up just where we left off. We make plans to keep in touch with him and his family about a foundation that we want to start that can be used to assist Iraqis in Iraq and the United States, our returning warriors, and several animal rescues both in the States and in the Middle East. The project is ambitious, and something that will keep us in close contact for the years to come, strengthening our forever bond.

The Mission Continues

It's early 2010 when I get an e-mail from Rich Crook. I quickly realize that this is different from our normal check-ins. It's a forwarded e-mail from a Navy SEAL named Todd, who is currently stationed in Afghanistan and looking into bringing a puppy home. "Look at this puppy, Carey," he writes. "Doesn't he look just like Boris?"

I quickly scan the e-mail for the picture and feel like I'm looking at a mirror image of Boris as a puppy: white and brown spots, rambunctious, and cute as a button. I read on, taking in the soldier's plea for help. Like Peter a few years before, he had what seemed like an impossible dream and was looking for someone who could help him make it happen.

Rich has let me know that he's not working for a group that can currently fund a rescue, but he's willing to help however he can. I look at the picture again, thinking of Boris and how lost I was when I was trying to figure out how to get him and Mama home. "Do you think it would be okay if I write to him and see what I can do?" I ask Rich, not knowing the first thing about what I'm going to say but feeling compelled to do it anyway.

"Can't hurt," Rich says.

So Todd and I start e-mailing back and forth, and I quickly get a sense of how much the puppy—whom he calls Tor, short for Torfan, from a local Kabul dialect and meaning "typhoon"—and the other dogs on the base mean to him. He tells me that he and his wife have been trying to figure out how to get the puppy back since it was born. Now, as the dog nears its six-month birthday, he knows that he is running out of options. The orders have come down for the troops to execute the dogs, and he has been able to hold them off for now, but knows he doesn't have much time left.

My experience with Mama and Boris turns out to be perfect training for this situation. The road map that Rich Crook helped me draw up is still fresh in my mind. In our e-mails back and forth, I identify the problems that we're going to have to overcome. We come up with a list of needs and places where we can start looking to get those needs met. I tell him about how we did it in Iraq and that we'll have to replicate the process as best we can in Afghanistan.

I use some of my contacts from Iraq to seek advice on where we should start in Afghanistan. Soon,

I'm talking to people at the airport. The dogs will have to fly from Afghanistan to Dubai on Safi Airways, the only commercial airline that flies in and out of Afghanistan. As with our mission in Iraq, the whole operation feels tenuous, patched together by kindness and chance. In the middle of a war zone, you rely on word of mouth to get you to the people you need to talk to—and sometimes, they're not so easy to find. There is an abstract level of trust that you have to will yourself to have when dealing with total strangers separated by continents and vast oceans, people who don't know the first thing about you, and who you don't know the first thing about. But I cross my fingers, hope that the universe and Peter will help guide me, and dive right in.

It turns out that Todd's wife has done a lot of volunteering in the animal rescue world, and so it is through her connections that we're able to receive funding from St. Louis Stray Rescue, an amazing organization. Like Best Friends, they run rescue operations in situations that can be complicated.

The one catch that we run into is that, like the rescue in Iraq, we will need someone to physically accompany the dogs from their connection in Dubai back to the United States. In Iraq, we had Rich Crook to fly in to the rescue, but there is no such luck at this time. We make contact with a woman who runs the kennel at the airport in Afghanistan to make sure that all the paperwork is in order and that the puppy will be walked and fed before getting on the plane—but that's where her help will end. We need someone to get on that plane.

I quickly volunteer my services. I've never been on a journey like that before, only having been outside of the country to visit Mexico and Canada. I know it will be an incredible experience, and to be able to help Todd bring his dog home will be reward enough. I pack lightly, as I'll be spending most of my time on planes and in airports, and off I go.

Once I'm on the plane, it becomes clear to me that I've been running on fumes. It has taken us nearly two months to get to this point, and I've spent my nights up in front of the computer and on the phone arranging the rescue operation. Totally exhausted, I can't seem to get my eyelids to shut—it's like all the adrenaline that I've been living off of for months has refused to quit, and my body has no intention of letting me sleep on this seemingly interminable flight. I watch the monitor on the seatback in front of me, following the plane icon as it moves across the map. Everyone else is asleep, and the cabin is quiet.

Suddenly, I realize that the plane is flying directly over Baghdad, a place that I have never been but that broke my heart all the same. Thankfully, the other passengers are passed out and don't see the small breakdown I have alone in my seat, sobbing for Peter, mourning his loss anew. It occurs to me that I am making the journey that I was supposed to make for Peter. I am now able to bring a puppy home that this soldier has bonded with, and now Todd will be able to have a new life with the puppy at home. It is such an honor to be part of this journey now, even if it's not for Peter's dogs. The emotions just hit me all at once, and I cry and cry until I finally fall asleep.

When I land in Dubai, there is too much to do for me to give in to any heartache that remains. I immediately go to the Delta desk, explain who I am, and request to go see that the puppy has been loaded onto the plane. The workers are polite with me, but firm. "I'm sorry, Ma'am, it's not possible for you to go down there."

I know that the rules are in place for very good reason, namely the security of the passengers. I try to be polite, but firm in response—not mean, but definitely more pushy than I'm used to being. I explain how far I've come and what I'm doing, and that I need to know that the dog is on the plane. This is my only mission in life at that moment.

One of the workers at the desk totally stuns me when he disappears with his cell phone and comes back with photos of Tor in his crate being loaded onto the plane. He leans across the counter to show me the pictures. I thank him profusely and send out a quick e-mail to everyone to let them know that I have Tor and we are heading back soon.

I'm only in the Dubai airport for an hour or so before I turn back around on a plane to Amsterdam, where once again I have to explain myself to the Delta ticket agents, who are as kind as they can be when dealing with a slightly hysterical, exhausted woman traveling with a dog she's never laid eyes on. They check and double-check the cargo hold, assuring me that Tor is inside. I put my trust in them and board the plane, which takes us back to Detroit. There, Todd's wife, Laura, waits with my mom to receive the puppy, and when I step out of the holding area with him, we all share a moment of tears of relief and happiness. I know that I have finally found a way to pay it forward, bolstered by the currents of generosity of those who did so much for me in my quest to bring Mama and Boris home.

Not much time passes before I get another e-mail from Todd, this one urgent and strained. He is thankful to me for bringing Tor home and sends me pictures that Laura has sent him of the puppy adjusting to his new home. But there is, it turns out, more to the mission than we originally thought.

"They're going to kill the other dogs," he says. "There are six of them. Is there anything you can do?"

I only have to think about it for about half a second before I write him back, saying yes, of course I will do anything I can. We had paved the way with Tor, and I feel confident that my connections, particularly the helpful people at the Delta counters, will be able to help me with whatever I need in the transition.

Fate plays more than a small hand in this decision, too, as it has with so many others throughout this journey. Just after I get back from my first trip to Dubai, I receive a small sum of money from Peter's life insurance policy. Most of it goes to my parents, but the amount that comes to me is substantial enough that it can be put to good use. The problem is, I want nothing to do with it. It feels like blood money to me—the only reason I have it is because Peter has died, and I am not about to go out and buy something with it. But as soon as I get this e-mail from Todd, I know that this is how I'm supposed to spend it. I know that this is what Peter would want.

I am worried about where we will place the dogs once we get them to the States, but Todd says not to worry about that part. He explains that each dog in the pack has a soldier who has really bonded with it, much like him and Tor, and has agreed to care for it. "They all have people who can meet you and take them off your hands when you come back," he explains. He says that Laura will come to pick up the mother of his puppy, a coincidence that makes me happy, having Mama and Boris at home.

This time, we don't have months to spend making arrangements. The orders for the pack's execution are imminent, and so the soldiers spring into action, making them crates and leashes and collars out of spare parts they find lying around, keeping them contained to receive their vaccines and keeping them out of harm's way. Within two weeks I'm back up in the air on my way to Dubai, ready to transport six dogs home for soldiers I've never met. It is another chance for me to be an angel for someone—several some-ones—and I love every moment of it.

The plan is more complicated than it was for Tor; there are regulations maintaining that only two dogs per ticket can be transported per flight from Kabul, and the airline only travels out of there once in the morning and once at night. We have timed my journey so that I will get there when the last dog arrives in Dubai, and then I can fly back with all six of them on the next flight out. Because I had a relatively easy time with Tor's transportation, though, I am feeling confident as I step off the plane and walk through the Jetway. That feeling is short-lived, though, as I see someone standing there with a sign on it bearing my name.

"What's going on?" I ask the woman.

"There are some problems," she says, and takes me up to Delta's lounge to explain.

In advance of the trip, I had put all of the money from the life insurance policy into my checking account so that the funds would be available immediately for all the tickets for the dogs, as well as my own ticket. However, in the midst of the transactions, my bank thought that the charges originating from Afghanistan and Dubai were fraudulent, and froze my account. While I was in the air on my sixteen-hour journey to Dubai without any way of communicating with the outside world, no one was able to reach me to take care of the problem, so four of the dogs are stuck in Kabul.

I make her repeat herself just to make sure I have the story straight. I am crestfallen as she confirms it: there are only two dogs here at this time. The staff in the lounge are very helpful and understanding, and give me Internet and phone access so that I can take care of the details with my bank. Once I've confirmed that the charges are not fraudulent, I am then able to call Safi and Delta and reschedule the flights for the other dogs. I go through a good round of nail biting while I make a decision between staying and waiting for the four dogs to arrive days later or taking off with the two I have now. Talking with Todd and Laura on the phone, we decide that it's best if I take off with the two dogs in the cargo hold now, and trust the gate agents at Delta—the same ones who were so helpful getting Tor home—to get them on the plane. Delta assures me again and again that they promise to get those dogs on the plane, and I put my faith in them.

The dogs and I go back through Amsterdam, and once I'm there, I present the gate agents with printouts for each dog with their name and a picture of them, as well as the time when they are expected to get in and what flight they should be booked out on. Everyone is very understanding and helpful, but it's hard not to be terrified, putting my faith in people to do the right thing for no reason other than that it's the right thing to do. I try to remind myself of the essential goodness of so many people I've met over the course of the past few years, and I step back on the plane and get home with the two dogs that I can help at the moment.

We have to rush Tor's mother from the airport as soon as we land in Detroit, though. The flight has almost killed her. She is severely dehydrated and malnourished, and the stress of the journey has been almost too much for her. Slowly, she perks up, responding to IV fluids that the vet administers. When things are looking like they are stable, I finally lie down for a few moments. It takes no time at all for me to fall asleep once I've hit the pillow.

Suddenly, before I know it, I'm awake again. It's dark outside, and I think I must be confused, off-kilter and off-schedule. I make a move to lie back down, but then I realize why I've gotten up in the first place: My phone is ringing. I stumble in the dark to pick it up. It's Todd's wife, Laura. Though her voice is calm and collected, she tells me that there's been a snag.

"A snag?" I ask, rubbing my eyes, worried that the dogs have gotten lost, missed their transfer, or one of the agents I spoke to disappeared and left an unhelpful, compassionless soul in his place. What could have possibly gone wrong?

I listen to what she's saying and then take the phone downstairs to turn on the news. I can hardly believe my eyes, and wonder if I'm still asleep and dreaming. A volcano in Iceland is erupting, plumes of ash and fire shooting up into the sky. Laura tells me that the entire world seems to be shutting down the airspace, particularly in Europe, where the dogs have their connecting flight. They aren't letting planes take off. I look at the clock, double-checking the time—it's near five A.M. "They should be gone or just leaving by now," I reassure her.

I hang up the phone with Laura and call Delta in Amsterdam. They quickly track the dogs down and confirm that they are on a plane sitting on the tarmac.

"Will they be able to take off?" I ask, praying to Peter and whoever else will listen to me.

"I don't know," the agent says, and promises to keep me updated.

The next three hours feel like an eternity. I can't sleep, so I pace around my living room, watching the news footage of Eyjafjallajökull spewing its innards skyward and disrupting travel plans the world over. I'm kicking myself for not staying with the dogs, thinking that even if I had been stuck for a month in Amsterdam because of the volcano, at least I'd be able to be with them. Who will take care of them? The newscasters say that it could be weeks before the airspace is opened back up. The worry gnaws at my gut until I finally get the call from Delta: The plane has been cleared for takeoff, and they'll be in the air soon.

It is one of the last planes to take off out of Amsterdam before they shut down the airport entirely.

"Peter, that was a close call," I say to the empty room, flopping on the couch and breathing a sigh of relief.

★ ★ ★

The dogs arrive the next day, clearly exhausted and confused but happy. I take them on a walk and provide some comfort and companionship while we wait for each soldier's family to drive or fly up to get their dogs. As I preside over the reunions, I marvel at this big world, how it works even when it seems like it doesn't, and even though we don't always necessarily understand the plan, it's there for all of us. The dogs all have huge personalities, and bound around the house and the yard like it's their own. While we're waiting, Todd sends news that he's finding ways to fund other rescues, and we provide a safe harbor for some of those dogs, too.

When you're going through a tragedy like the one we experienced, it's easy to hate the universe, to think it exists only to cause you harm. But with each dog that comes off a plane in Detroit on its way to its new home with a soldier it helped heal in some way, I understand more and more that the universe can be a fundamentally good place. The experience is incredible and restores my faith in humanity. This is especially true of one dog in particular—a small, sick puppy with a mottled coat of brown and gold.

The puppy is supposed to go on to St. Louis, to a soldier's family there, but we keep her as she recuperates. She is eventually well enough to be vaccinated properly, and shockingly gets along well with Mama and Boris. Mama, in particular, accepts her as if she were one of her own puppies. The soldier who is slated to take the puppy, though, doesn't seem so excited anymore—her communications have grown ambivalent and clouded. She seems unsure that anyone will be able to care for the dog while it waits for her to come home.

I reach out to Todd to ask him to help grease the wheels. When he writes back to say that the soldier can't take the dog, I immediately know what to do. She will stay with us.

We name her Razia, a Dhari word which means chosen, or happy.

Afterword

So that Others May Stand Free

Before I took my first flight as an angel for someone else, before my heart heals, there is more reckoning to live through.

About nine months after Peter's death, the Army releases its findings from their investigation. We get messages on the home phone saying that we have to drive into downtown Detroit to pick up a letter that they've tried to deliver to us a couple times, but that no one was home to sign for. Nervous and agitated, we make the trip downtown to pick up the mysterious envelope, which features hand-written warnings about not opening alone. We can't imagine what awful things are inside.

Inside is a toxicology report, saying that Peter had various drugs in his system that could have interacted with one another, forming a deadly cocktail in his

bloodstream. They found copious amounts of Benadryl, which Peter would take to help him fall asleep,
as well as trace amounts of antibiotics and other drugs.

To say this is shocking is an understatement. There
is still not a word that I can find to describe the feeling of hearing that information. It feels so stupid, and
pointless, and so incredibly sad. I think back to con-
versations I've had with his friends on base who said
that they heard him snoring loudly the night he passed
away, and that they couldn't believe he was gone when
they woke up—the snoring had been such a normal
sign of life. Now, with this information, if it's true,
I realize that it was more likely that they heard Peter fighting for his life, choking to death on his own
vomit. We just can't believe that it ended this way. That
Peter would survive life in a war zone, but not in his
own bed.

I dig into the report, eager for more answers, for
anything that will allow me to understand this information and assimilate it with what I know. I quickly
find that there is no way. Inconsistencies pop up, and
I make phone calls about them. If he died in his sleep,
I ask, why was he intubated? Why did it say that there
was an IV inserted in his arm?

More information comes out—his bunkmates
found him in the morning, saw that he had vomit and
blood around his mouth, and carried him out on a
backboard to the medic tent, where they tried to re-

vive him. At the medic tent, though he was unrespon-
sive, he still had a pulse, and they had tried to stabilize
him for 20 minutes before they lost him. The medic
tent is equipped for the traumas of war, not the mysterious strangleholds of anaphylactic shock, which Peter
was exhibiting. He was officially pronounced dead at
6:17 A.M. There was no evidence of foul play.

Still, I can't believe what I've read in the toxicology report, and since there was no blood available after
it was drained from his body, we couldn't include a
blood panel in our private autopsy. I read the reports,
both of them, over again.

I get on the phone with the soldiers from his unit,
and they reassure me that they saw Peter take nothing. That he had never acted strangely. That everything
was normal. I inquire into the reports of a rash found
in the autopsy, a small bump behind his ear, and get no
definitive answers. He could have had an allergic reac-
tion to an insect bite, they concede, but it's nothing
conclusive, either way.

I turn things over in my mind, small moments that
meant nothing at the time. How I bothered Peter to
get his sleep apnea checked out but he wouldn't. How
some soldiers had told me that they heard him breathing erratically. That he had asthma. All of these things
could have contributed to his death. I am confident
that there was nothing he would have willingly done
to put his life—or his standing in the Army—at risk.

So I grasp at more straws, look for more answers.

There is a photograph of a single pill included in the report, a small tablet that was found in Peter's things when he died. It was not in a prescription bottle, and the Army doctors say they don't know what it is. I show the picture to his bunkmates, who say they've never seen it before. I spend hours on the Internet, in libraries, looking through drug books. I call pharmaceutical companies. I see pharmacists. I try every road I can, every avenue I can think of. I obsess for over a year about this pill, trying to identify it and come up with a reason why Peter had it. I get nowhere.

I keep returning to the toxicology report, which lists "mixed drug interaction" as the cause of death. But after all my research, after the Army's investigation, and after a private autopsy, we are no closer to finding the answers. I know, not firsthand, but from the few times I heard Peter talk about it, the incredible amount of stress that soldiers are under. I know the John McCain quote my father often referenced, about how bad things happen during war. I know from looking in his eyes how much war changed him, how it scarred him inside. I know from talking to him how his insomnia wreaked havoc on his body, and that he took Benadryl to help him drift off to sleep, and I know that people are fragile—that this pill and that pill can be innocuous in the hand, and deadly in the gut. But I also know that he was a good man, and a strong man. Could he have succumbed to that pressure, wanted to numb the pain, take the edge off one night? It's possible. Could that Benadryl that he had to take to dull the nightmares that kept him awake at night have caused his death? It's possible.

Anything is possible, but none of it matters.

At Peter's memorial service, my father delivered a touching eulogy through a torrent of tears. It was beautiful at the time, but now, after all of this agonizing, all of this searching, all of this pain wrought by circumstances we'll never fully understand, it carries so much more meaning.

Peter was a soldier. And I ask you, does it matter how a soldier dies? Is it less glorious to have starved or froze to death, to die of pestilence or simple accident? To be shot, blown up or burned? No. It does not matter how a soldier dies. Because dying is what a soldier commits to do. But dying is not what a soldier is. A soldier is one who stands while others hide. He moves forward while others turn away. A soldier retreats, but only to regain the advantage. He is the one who stands in harm's way so that others may stand free and safe. A soldier seeks to harm only to stop the harm. He kills only to stop the killing. And he often dies a hellish death, yet his soul does not dwell in such places. He is our protector in this strange uncertainness in which we live. And I cannot

pretend to understand what has happened, nor could
I have stopped it or changed it in any way.

I reach a breaking point after a year of searching for the identity of the mysterious pill. Or maybe it's better to call it a breakthrough. I realize that what I wanted more than anything, the only thing I wanted, was to have Peter back. That's what I was chasing for all of those hours in front of the computer, in all of those phone calls to experts, to the Army. I was trying to strike an impossible bargain: I wanted my brother back. And I could never have him: he's gone forever. I know in my heart that, no matter what I turn up, it's not going to bring him back.

But there is another side to this coin. The other side is this: No matter what I turn up or don't turn up, it doesn't mar his memory; it doesn't dilute his sacrifice. I know that he did not plan on leaving us that night, that whatever events conspired to take him from us, it was nothing more than a tragic accident. I realize that if there's anything I need to hold on to, it's not how Peter died, however that may have been. It's how he lived.

How You Can Help

There are a few organizations I would like to recommend if you would like to help.

The first one is the Sgt Peter C. Neesley Foundation. This is a non-profit organization that was founded by myself and Dan Fontella. This umbrella non-profit will be used in several ways to benefit the many people who help make miracles continue to happen in both Iraq and the United States. One hundred percent of the donations will go to many worthy causes. To find further information and to donate please go to www. sgtpeterneesley.com.

Another very worthy organization is the Puppy Rescue Mission. This organization formed right around the same time that I was doing the rescues in Afghanistan. This organization has now rescued hundreds of dogs and cats our soldiers have adopted on the battlefield. They raise most of their funds via Facebook. If you would like to help bring our soldiers' battle buddies home, please visit them at www.the-puppyrescuemission.org.

Also visit Rich Crook's non-profit, Grassroots Emergency Animal Rescue, on Facebook and find out how you can help in animal rescues worldwide.

I would also recommend two very special animal rescue organizations, the Best Friends Animal Society, at www.bestfriends.org, and the St. Louis Stray Rescue, at www.strayrescue.org. Both of these organizations provide exceptional service to our furry friends and arrange for forever homes for homeless dogs, cats, and other animals.

Acknowledgements

There are stars whose radiance is visible on Earth though they have long been extinct. There are people whose brilliance continues to light the world though they are no longer among the living. These lights are particularly bright when the night is dark. They light the way for humankind.

—Hannah Senesh, poet, playwright,
and paratrooper (1921–44)

I am going to do my best to put into words things that simply cannot be expressed with words alone. This book was a dream that I had after Mama and Boris's journey concluded. I wanted to write it as a means to share with the world the results of its generous actions. As a way to spread my brother's legacy and the unlikely miracles that sprung from tragedy. A way to pay homage to my brother's never-ending love and continued protection. And a way to say thank you to everyone involved in making this miracle come true.

This book was written from my memory and I hope I did the story justice, for each of you played an important role. And without each one of you and your unwavering efforts, this story would never have come to pass, let alone be made public. What I owe you is a debt that can never be repaid. I love you all.

I want to begin by thanking my son, Patrick Peter Neesley. We make a great team, kiddo. Thank you for your patience and love. You will forever be my sunshine. I would also like to thank my fiancé, the love of my life, Dan Fontella. Your love and support mean everything to me. Thank you for putting up with my crazy life. I would also like to thank my parents, Robert "Spike" Neesley, Jr. and Christine Neesley. My bonus mom, Ann Neesley. My brother Ted Neesley and "surrogate" brothers, Marty Finkelmeier and Evan Perri, for keeping me balanced and continuing to find ways to keep Peter's spirit alive. My soul sisters, Suzie Bianco Broadrick, Carrie Moloney Kirby and Terri Kirk, I never would have survived this without you. Also, thank you to all my extended family and friends. Many of you assisted in this miracle and without your support to keep me grounded, I may have lost my mind!

I would like to thank my military family, who came to me in my darkest days. The soldiers who served alongside my brother, you are family for life now. In particular: Daniel Haynes, Mark Hookano and Erik Torres. The three of you took care of my brother's dogs after he left us. In all your grief, you stood up and continued to carry on for Peter and to assist us in ways no one else could. You are forever in my heart. Also Mike Keen and Erik "KJ" Kjonnerod, whose strong guidance and love for my brother was evident. Your continued presence in our lives is a precious lifeline to Peter. I would also like to take this space to remember the two other soldiers who were lost during Peter's unit's deployment to Iraq. On July 6, 2007, the world lost two incredible warriors. May we always remember Gene Lamie and LeRon Wilson and their surviving family and friends. And a very special thank you to all the Gold Star families who have reached out to us in our most desperate time and offered a kind ear. Your love and support is invaluable.

I would like to thank Rich Crook and the Best Friends Animal Society, without whom none of this would ever have been possible. Not only did you provide us with an invaluable resource and support through your international rescue network, but you also funded the rescue. Rich Crook, you will never convince me that you are anything less than an angel sent directly from Peter to make an impossible journey possible. Your unwavering dedication and commitment, as well as your uplifting spirit, gave me strength where I was sure I had none left. Rich has moved on from Best Friends, and is currently working with the United States Humane Society and teaching others how to set up Rapid Response Animal Rescue during times of disaster, as well as Spay and Neuter Programs,

TNR programs, and education on animal welfare in general. He is also starting up a non-profit based in Michigan called Grassroots Emergency Animal Rescue (GEAR). He continues to remain a precious asset to all our furry friends. And a special thank you to Best Friends photographer, Molly Wald, whose gentle soul and beautiful talent captured Mama and Boris from the moment they hit U.S. soil to our home. Your pictures stand as a constant reminder of the miracles that we were given. Also, a special thank you to Best Friends' staff writer, Cathy Scott, who retold our journey with amazing talent and grace, and assisted me in my beginning writing process and answered tons of questions for me. All your support helped to keep things in perspective.

I would like to thank John Wagner and Gryphon Airlines for their part in our journey. The air transportation was a huge hurdle, one we thought we would wrestle with for quite some time. And you came out of nowhere with the offer of help and crossed one of our biggest challenges off our list. You are truly another one of our angels. And John did not stop there—he has continued to offer assistance in Afghanistan—his knowledge and help has been priceless as we continue to assist other organizations to help soldiers rescue their battle buddies and get them home to the U.S.

A very special thank you to the Al Murrani family. Here there truly are no words. Each one of you is a precious gift that I will never ever forget. You truly fell from Heaven into our lives. I will spend the rest of my life in deepest gratitude to each one of you. You are family.

Thank you to Gerard Righetti, Peter Ransby and each member of Iraq's elite team from Threat Management Group. Your kindness and precious knowledge of the country and ability to maneuver within its difficult security checkpoints were an invaluable key to our success. Your persistence and ability to persevere held us together.

This task would have been a much bigger challenge without the efforts of Senator Carl Levin and his former assistant Justin Harlem. They took an immediate interest in our story and their connections with the Department of Defense were the key to passing through the myriad of security checkpoints. The assistance they provided with the CDC was also much appreciated. They assisted in making the miles of red tape manageable, and had us perfectly prepared for a seamless clearance. I would also like to thank former Michigan Governor Jennifer Granholm and her assistant, Linda Droste. Their assistance was also priceless.

And I also owe a debt to the local and national media whose persistence is what sparked the idea to let this story out and let the world in to help. Without the exposure, we never would have found our angels. And to all the people who sent us a note, a suggestion, a prayer—we read every one. You gave us strength and encouragement to keep fighting another day.

I would also like to thank the Grosse Pointe community for all their support. The Grosse Pointe Farms and Park Police Departments that escorted and protected us. The War Memorial, and President, Dr. Mark Weber, that sheltered us. Verheyden's Funeral Home and owner Brian Joseph who helped us honor Peter and his life. The Patriot Guard Riders who held us and shielded us throughout the painful process of saying goodbye. The Honor Guard from Fort Knox, who stayed with our family and Peter. You were a constant reminder of Peter's larger family, who were also grieving. Your sensitivity, respect, commitment, and love were invaluable.

Also I would like to thank Banfield Pet Hospital in Chesterfield, Michigan, for assistance in the first year of care and recovery for Mama and Boris, as well as Harper Woods Vets, who have continued to care for my special babies. And Platz Animal Hospital in Grosse Pointe that assisted us with our Afghanistan rescues. The Invisible Fence Company that insured my feral newcomers did not escape from our yard. And to animal trainers Joel Silverman and Jim Lessenberry, who helped me to train and socialize Mama and Boris. And Jim and his company Animal Learning Systems, who helped to train Razia as well.

Finally, I need to thank Michael Levin, Sara Stratton, and Jenn Salcido from Business Ghost. Michael, you took a chance on me and my story. You listened for an entire day as I poured this story and my heart out to you. And you believed in this story. I can't thank you and your talented and caring staff enough. I would also like to thank Jill Marsal, my very talented literary agent. And of course, thanks to Reader's Digest for seeing the beauty in our story and in my brother's life.

To all my readers—I really hope that this story touches your heart and makes you believe in miracles.

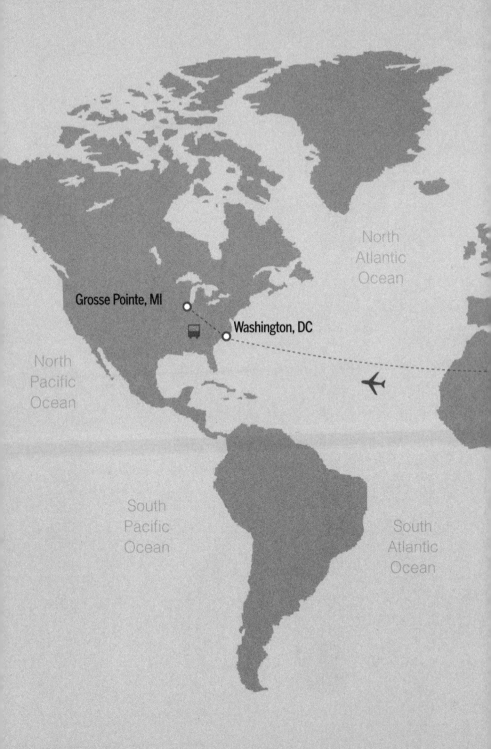